HONDA

THE GOLDEN AGE

ISLE OF MAN **TT**™ 1959–67

MATTHEW RICHARDSON

PEN & SWORD
TRANSPORT
AN IMPRINT OF PEN & SWORD BOOKS LTD.
YORKSHIRE - PHILADELPHIA

First published in Great Britain in 2024 by
Pen and Sword Transport
An imprint of
Pen & Sword Books Ltd.
Yorkshire - Philadelphia

ISBN 978 1 39905 147 7

A CIP catalogue record for this book is available from the British Library.

Typeset in 12/16 pt Palatino
Typeset by SJmagic DESIGN SERVICES, India.
Printed and bound in the UK by CPI Group (UK) Ltd.

Pen & Sword Books Ltd incorporates the imprints of Pen & Sword Books Archaeology, Atlas, Aviation, Battleground, Discovery, Family History, History, Maritime, Military, Naval, Politics, Railways, Select, Transport, True Crime, Fiction, Frontline Books, Leo Cooper, Praetorian Press, Seaforth Publishing, Wharncliffe and White Owl.

For a complete list of Pen & Sword titles please contact

PEN & SWORD BOOKS LIMITED
George House, Units 12 & 13, Beevor Street, Off Pontefract Road, Barnsley, S71 1HN, UK
E-mail: enquiries@pen-and-sword.co.uk
Website: www.pen-and-sword.co.uk

or

PEN AND SWORD BOOKS
1950 Lawrence Rd, Havertown, PA 19083, USA
E-mail: uspen-and-sword@casematepublishers.com
Website: www.penandswordbooks.com

MIX
Paper | Supporting responsible forestry
FSC® C013604

HONDA
THE GOLDEN AGE

ISLE OF MAN **TT**™ 1959–67

CONTENTS

ACKNOWLEDGEMENTS

The core of this book grew from research that I carried out in 2009 for a museum exhibition that marked the fiftieth anniversary of Honda's first venture into Grand Prix motorcycle racing, at the 1959 Isle of Man TT races. The further I looked into this story the more fascinating I found it, for it had more than a single engineering or racing dimension. There was a great deal of social history woven into it; for example the story of Japan's incredible economic miracle in rebuilding its industry from the ashes of total defeat in the Second World War, and also the resurrection of Anglo-Japanese relations that had hit rock bottom during those years. Then there was the character of Soichiro Honda. No one could fail to be impressed by the determination of this man, and his achievement in building one of the world's largest corporations virtually from nothing. Then there were the riders, charismatic figures like Mike Hailwood, whose stories cried out to be documented.

I received a great deal of help in 2009, from a number of different sources. The Honda company provided me with information and contacts. The late Don Simons provided me with other information from Japan. Local enthusiasts, such as John Dalton, were of enormous help in sharing their knowledge of the machines and their riders. John also supplied some of the photographs that appear herein. TT supporters who had been children at the time of the Japanese arrival sent me their memories of this extraordinary meeting of cultures – I am particularly grateful to Roy Moore and the late Adrian Earnshaw in this respect. Neil Hanson also offered his perspective on various events, for which I thank him.

Bill Snelling as ever was helpful with photographs from his expansive archive, and once again I am grateful to the late Ken Sprayson, who allowed me access to his wonderfully evocative collection of photographs. Lisa Noakes kindly allowed me to use a rare photograph from the collection of her late uncle Nigel McClatchey. Iris Burden similarly allowed me to use a photo from the collection of her late husband. Mr J.A. Ranscombe allowed me to use material from the Ranscombe archive, for which I thank him sincerely. Wendy Thirkettle in the MNH library assisted me with images once again. Former riders Jim Redman and Tommy Robb sent me memories and insights that were invaluable. I am particularly grateful also to the late Naomi Taniguchi for consenting to be interviewed about his memories of Honda and the Isle of Man, and to Unno San for facilitating this for me in Japan. In the Isle of Man, Mark Watterson and Rob Teare offered generous help in translating this material, and I thank all of these people for assisting in what is believed to be the first personal account from this Japanese rider to be presented in English. Likewise, my thanks go to Simon Crellin at the Isle of Man Government Motorsport Office for assistance with use of the TT trademark.

At Honda in the UK Iain Baker was particularly helpful in securing permission for me to use material and I thank him warmly for this. However, logos, model names and designations have been used in this book solely for the purposes of identification, illustration and decoration and remain the property of the trademark holder. Finally, Ted Macauley, the veteran former *Daily Mirror* journalist, was kind enough to allow me to quote some passages from his book *Hailwood,* for which I am immensely grateful. As on many occasions previously, he was unstinting in his generosity and helped my work enormously. I hope that this meets your eye, Ted.

As ever, any errors of fact or interpretation are of course my own.

Matthew Richardson
Douglas, Isle of Man 2023

INTRODUCTION

The story of Honda's arrival at the TT is the stuff of legend, but it bears retelling here. Soichiro Honda, the visionary founder of the Japanese motor company, had set his sights on breaking into the European motorcycle market, and reasoned that the best way to prove his machines was through racing success, at the Isle of Man TT. Amazingly it took him only four years to turn that ambition (which to many observers seemed so unlikely) into reality. It is said that nothing succeeds like success, and in a few short years he had built upon his achievements to make Honda Motor a global super company.

Soichiro Honda had been a motorcar racer in his native Japan in the 1930s, but he was also an astute and innovative businessman. He would found a number of companies during his lifetime, but as he later freely admitted, not all of them were successful; during the Second World War he ran a firm producing piston rings for aircraft engines, but following the defeat of Japan he sold the business. In 1948, he started a new venture fitting war surplus engines into bicycle frames, and called it the Honda Motor Company.

Japanese goods had a poor reputation in the 1950s, and were often viewed as inferior copies of western products. Indeed, it is fair to say that in the immediate post-war years Honda's first machines were not spectacular. However, Soichiro needed to overcome negative perceptions and the best way to do that would be to prove the quality of his products in the toughest environment of all. He came to the Isle of Man TT – the pinnacle of motorcycle racing – in 1954, and vowed that the next year a Honda team would be back and that they would win. In fact, it was 1959 before a Honda factory team made it to the Island. By 1967, they had won everything that there was to win on two wheels.

In those years, the Isle of Man TT was the British round of the Motorcycle World Championship, a glamorous circus that saw race teams move from circuit to circuit, across Europe, the Far East and the Americas each year as they sought the glory that came with victory at the highest level. This was a high-octane, high-pressure environment, in which a factory ride was the ultimate ambition of every teenage racer who started out in motorcycle sport. The greatest and most prestigious factory team of them all was Honda.

This is the story of that first tentative foray into motorcycle racing, and of the spectacular successes that followed. It will examine the stories of the Honda machines that became legendary, and of the men who made them legends. The Isle of Man TT was already a storied event when Honda came to it; throughout the Twenties, Thirties and Fifties it had produced legendary riders, bore witness to thrilling battles and had made the names of countless marques. But Honda's arrival and their achievements wrote a new chapter in that story, which still captures the imagination of anyone who loves motorcycles even today.

Chapter One

1954–59
HONDA'S DREAM

Soichiro Honda was born in 1906, in a small rural village near the city of Hamamatsu, Japan. His father was a blacksmith, and he grew up amid the smoke from the forge and the sound of the anvil. He enjoyed watching machinery pound and twist pieces of metal into new shapes. He recalled later:

> If I remember correctly it was at the age of four or five that I first began to take an interest in engines. There was a rice milling plant a few miles from my home and it had a diesel engine, which fascinated me. I watched endlessly as the engine operated in a cloud of exhaust fumes and a clatter of noise. When I was in the second grade, the first motor car came to our village. It had a folding roof and I followed it hastily. When the car stopped, it leaked a considerable amount of oil on the ground. The smell of the oil has always enchanted me, and I literally put my nose to the ground and breathed in deeply.[1]

At school Honda performed poorly, and although he was interested in science lessons that covered batteries, test tubes and machines, reading and writing he thought tedious. During these lessons he would often be found on a nearby hill, daydreaming. Consequently he did poorly in exams. By the time Honda left school aged sixteen, he had secured an apprenticeship at the Art Trading Company, one of the few automobile repair shops in Tokyo. About eighteen months after he joined, the city was levelled by the great earthquake of 1923. With the city in flames, the master ordered all of his apprentices who could drive to get in a car and take it to a safe place. Honda jumped behind the wheel of a vehicle that was in for repair and safely navigated the debris and fleeing pedestrians to get the car away. It was the first time he had ever actually driven an automobile. After the earthquake, Art Trading was busy repairing cars that had been damaged in the fire. During this time, Honda rode a motorcycle for the first time when his boss sent him out on a sidecar combination carrying messages around the city. He remembered:

> Driving a car for the first time, riding around on a motorcycle and learning how to repair automobiles – for me the great earthquake was nearly a blessing.[2]

By the time Honda was twenty-two, so great was his master's confidence in him that he allowed him to set up his own branch of Art Trading in Hamamatsu. Soon he had a reputation as the best repair shop in the area. At the same time, his master was becoming interested in racing cars, and persuaded him to build him a bespoke machine. Honda took a 90hp Curtis aircraft engine from a flying school and mounted it in an Oakland automobile chassis. It was a steep learning curve for the young engineer:

> As soon as the engine was started, oil fouled the plugs. Since I had no knowledge about changing the type of plug at that time, I struggled hard to alter the crank case and make other changes to stop the oil from flooding the plugs.[3]

However, he overcame these difficulties and on a trial run at a Tokyo airfield the machine achieved 100kph, which was impressive for those days. The machine went on to win races, which encouraged Honda to build further racing cars and enter them in competitions himself. He achieved several wins, but his racing days came to a sudden halt when he was only thirty-one years of age. During the All-Japan Automobile Speed Championships he was driving a supercharged Ford four, with the engine tilted by 10 degrees in the frame to give stability on the oval course. Honda was in the process of setting a new Japanese speed record of 120kph when another car pulled out of the pits directly in front of him. Both he and his brother who was a passenger were almost killed when their car went end over end three times. He was awarded the trophy for the new lap record, but when he got out of hospital he turned his attention to a new venture, manufacturing piston rings.

However, this was not as straightforward as he might have imagined. He could not sell them as they were so poor. Out of a first batch of 30,000 he selected fifty for testing, and only three passed as acceptable. With the company facing bankruptcy he enrolled in classes at the local technical high school to learn the intricacies of casting. When he showed the teachers one of his piston rings, one of them observed there was not enough silicone in them; bemused, Honda replied that he was not even aware silicone was necessary! However, nine months after enrolling he was turning out good piston rings.

During the Second World War his company supplied the Japanese army, navy and air force, but 1945 found the country in ruins following defeat by the Allies. Honda's main market had now gone, but in a tiny 12ft by 18ft shack on a bomb-levelled site he began a new venture, with a rickety, belt-driven lathe and a few salvaged work desks and chairs. He now bought 500 cheap war surplus two-stroke motors and fitted them to bicycles as a low-cost form of transport. His output was low at first, with only one machine a day produced. Gasoline was also in short supply, and the engines were modified to run on a foul-smelling concoction derived from pine-tree roots. They also had to be pedalled furiously before the engine would catch and start. However, in war-ravaged Japan, with little or no public transport, overcrowded trains and buses and taxis powered by charcoal burners, these were enormously popular. When he sold the first 500 he set about building his own engines to fit to bicycles; Honda came up with the 50cc 'Chimney' engine, so-called because of the odd, protruding cylinder head. However, the performance was not bad for those days, and the two-stroke engine, refined as the 'A Type', produced ½hp. Production now could not keep up with demand, and so in 1948 Honda Motor Company Limited was born, with a capital of $2,777 and thirty-four employees, about three times as many as the original shack had contained.

At this time there were eight motorcycle producers in Japan, but none manufactured both the frames and the engines. Honda became the first manufacturer to achieve this in August 1949 when it put the D-type engine into its own frame. The two-stroke, single-cylinder engine developed an impressive 2.3hp, which was fed through a two-gear transmission and chain. The frame was a pressed steel channel type. Mr Honda said of it:

> With this, my dream has come true.[4]

So the machine was christened the Honda Dream. It was very popular and models were selling as fast as they could be made. In 1950 the company opened an office in Tokyo, and with a loan from the Japanese government was able to invest in new equipment that put their output up to 300 units a month.

So successful was the company that in 1952 Mr Honda was awarded a Blue Ribbon Medal in recognition of his innovation and his contribution to rebuilding the Japanese economy. As the award was to be made personally by the Emperor, a government official contacted Honda to advise him on the protocol for the occasion. When told that he must appear in a formal morning coat and pinstriped trousers, he replied:

> Are you kidding? Our work uniform is good enough. I don't even own a suit, much less a black tie outfit. If I have to wear a morning coat, I don't want the medal.[5]

He was eventually persuaded to borrow a suit for the occasion, but the incident provides a vivid illustration of Honda's character, and showed that he was more comfortable on the shop floor alongside his employees than with mixing in high society. Despite the success of Honda Motor Company in the domestic market, the firm was little known outside of Japan, but Honda's ambition knew no bounds. In October of that year he made a speech to motorcycle dealers and the general public in Japan:

> It has been my long-cherished hope to delight customers with good products at low prices, but I am not yet satisfied either as regards performance or price. In the past I have purchased the best machinery produced by Japan's top makers to equip productive factories, but now we have reached the limit imposed by this machinery. My company has become, in name and in fact, the leader of the Japanese motorcycle industry.

> We have gone well ahead of the others in both the performance of our products and production. We have become number one in Japan, but looking at the rest of the world can make you embarrassed with our present level. My aim is to make products even better than the current world level.[6]

His vision led him to import the best available American, German and Swiss automatic lathes and machine tools, items that could massively improve productivity in his factories. It was costly, and a gamble, but Soichiro Honda believed that a greater risk lay in standing still and potentially being overtaken by a competitor. The reality of the situation, however, was Honda's rapid growth had plateaued. Rapid expansion had come at the expense of reliability and the company's reputation – and sales figures – had suffered as a result. Author Tetsuo Sakiya attributes at least part of this to Soichiro's brash leadership style, and goes on to say:

> Because of the company's rapid growth following the success of the Dream Type E, over 2,000 new workers had been hired. They differed greatly both in terms of ability and salaries, which caused some confusion in the internal organisation of the factory. Honda appeared almost every day to supervise his engineers, and his behaviour was often abrasive and sometimes violent when he was not satisfied with their work. For their part, some of the workers were disappointed in the 'management style' of their boss and began to have doubts about the future of the company. The morale at Honda Motor was plummeting and incidents of sabotage were reported.[7]

Honda needed a distraction urgently, not least to draw the attention of domestic banks away from the company balance sheet. In March 1954, he announced that the firm would be entering the Isle of Man TT Races. He believed that he would have to beat the best foreign machines on their home ground if he was to have any chance of breaking into those markets. Honda was also aware, however, that developing a successful reputation in racing could transform his brand. He remembered:

> Most of the workers were so young that they were quite attracted to the idea of winning races, particularly because we had just lost the war, the idea of hoisting the Japanese flag on the Isle of Man gave them much excitement. It really stirred their blood.[8]

Accordingly, Honda went to see the TT races in June of that year, but was shocked at what he found. European racing machines were turning out three times as much power as Honda's machines of the same size. Commentator Murray Walker remembered encountering the Japanese party in that year:

> The Japanese were not flavour of the year, never mind flavour of the month in 1954 because it was only nine years after the end of the war, and that's not a very long time, and we'd had these dreadful atrocities against our troops during the war, and this was the first appearance they made, and it was the first time that any of us had ever seen a Japanese, so they came over with a bit of a cloud hanging over them, but there were some, and I think I must have been one of them, who thought

> well, you know, the war's over now, and turn the other cheek ... You would go up to these people and, adopting the time-honoured British procedure of speaking to foreigners slowly and loud, you would say:
>
> 'WHERE... ARE... YOU... FROM...?'
> 'Honda Motor Company.'
> 'WHAT? OH, HONDA. AND ... WHAT ... DO ... YOU ... DO ...?'
> 'We make motorcycle.'
> 'OH, YOU MAKE MOTORCYCLES? WHY ARE YOU HERE?'
> 'Next year we come TT Races.'
> 'NEXT YEAR TT RACES? WITH A KAMIKAZE SPECIAL MAYBE? AND WHO WILL RIDE FOR YOU? HARRY KARI, WILL HE RIDE?'
>
> And we all thought this was very funny, you see, anti-Japanese jokes ...[9]

For the next few years, smartly dressed and impeccably mannered Japanese observers would be evident among the regular TT trippers and holidaymakers on the Isle of Man each summer. They were always to be found at the best viewing spots and were always festooned with the latest products of Japanese industry – cameras and audio tape recorders, the latter with which to better analyse engine revolutions and gear ratios.

Realising that they had a considerable amount of work to do in order to be competitive, they went home and set to work. The Honda technicians purchased examples of the European machines that were dominating racing at that time, such as an NSU and an FB Mondial. They took these machines apart and studied them carefully, not with a view to copying them but to understand how these engines were able to produce so much more power than Honda's own at that time. Along the way they made an important discovery. Conventional wisdom had it that two valves per cylinder provided optimal performance. However, Honda decided to experiment with four valves, with dramatic results. Engineering journalist Kevin Cameron explains:

> Every dimension of the single, larger valve is bigger. Its head diameter is bigger, so the head must also be thicker to support combustion pressure over its larger area. The bigger valve needs a longer valve stem, to make room for its larger single port to turn down, and that stem has to be sufficiently thicker to withstand the force of the stronger valve springs. It's like comparing two cubes, one whose sides are 1 inch long, and another whose sides are 2 inches long. What is the ratio of their volumes? For the 1-inch cube, it's 1 cubic inch: 1 × 1 × 1 = 1. But for the 2-inch cube, it is 2 × 2 × 2 = 8 cubic inches.
>
> Instead of scaling directly with head diameter, valve weight scales nearly as the cube of head diameter. The lighter the valve, the easier it is to make it follow the cam contour without valve float.
>
> So here was a solution – provided adequate flow could be achieved. Choosing to build a four-valve-per-cylinder engine reduced valve weight enough that Honda could safely operate the valve train at engine speeds roughly 40 per cent higher.
>
> Getting adequate flow turned out to be a non-problem. All Honda had to do was make the cylinder's bore slightly greater than the piston's stroke. This gave enough room for four valves big enough to supply all the airflow they

> needed – even though four-valve's specific airflow is less than that of a well-designed two-valve engine.[10]

One other area upon which they chose to focus was combustion. At that time no one, neither universities nor the major automobile manufacturers in the United States, were looking seriously at this area. It was just assumed to be a given, and no one even questioned if it could be made more efficient, but Honda had noticed that analysis of exhaust gases showed quantities of unburned hydro-carbons and carbon monoxide. He set his Research and Development lab onto analysing every stage by which the fuel and air mixture came into contact with the spark plug, and how the mixture burned. His scientists discovered that the configuration of the combustion chamber had a huge influence over the process, and were able to develop one that maximised the power gained from the fuel.

Other technical issues also had to be overcome; Honda's early flywheels had a tendency to disintegrate at very high revs, with fragments bursting through the engine casing and embedding themselves in the ceiling. Clearly this would be catastrophic in a race situation, but engineers struggled to overcome the problem until Soichiro brought some of the knowledge of metal casting from his piston ring days to the equation. He pointed out that any defect in the outer casing of the flywheel would result in failure at very high speed, so the component was completely redesigned. They also reasoned that saving weight was as important as gaining power, so they lightened components where they could, for example on the connecting rod. They also worked to develop in-house a lighter, stronger chain that was more durable than anything else available on the Japanese domestic market at that time.

The designs for the engine to be used in the TT races were drawn up by two of the youngest engineers on Honda's staff, Tadashi Kume and Kimio Shimmura. The president believed that younger people were more flexible in their thinking and were less likely to be trapped in established patterns of doing things. However, entrusting such an important task to relative novices was unquestionably a gamble. The success or failure of the engine that they developed could set the course for the entire company. In many ways, this was another example of Soichiro Honda's unorthodox approach: most Japanese companies were strictly hierarchical and for them such an important job would have been given to the most senior engineers. For their part, the two young engineers appreciated the faith that their boss had in them, remembering:

> We were told to start designing racing engines right after we joined the company. Nothing could have been more interesting, and we were both very excited. If we had gone to another company, we never would have been given such challenging jobs.[11]

Soichiro Honda appreciated the efforts of the young designers, continuing:

> Nearly two years after we declared our intention to take part in the Isle of Man races, as the technical levels and mechanical features of the engine improved, we were able to come up with an engine powerful enough to compete with foreign motorcycles. The young engineers did a very good job. But that alone was not enough to assure us victory in the Tourist Trophy races. The rider is as important as the machine. Even if we had a machine with the same level of performance as those of our

> competitors, we still couldn't win the race without a top-notch rider. We had to develop a racing machine with a superior performance that would win even without a superior rider.[12]

Even so, Honda also sought to develop a stable of young riders to race his machines, and this was something that he had to build from scratch, as there was no body of experienced racers in Japan from which to draw as there was in Europe. One of these young riders was Naomi Taniguchi, an eager lad from a humble background, who had been born in the suburbs of Tokyo. Like many other Japanese of his generation, his father had been killed in the war, and he left school without much in the way of qualifications. He remembered:

> When I was sixteen I went to an employment exchange at Idabashi and they said they had something which would suit a young, keen and fun-loving fellow like me. I took public transport to Honda's factory, which looked old-fashioned, as they all did then. I wasn't even sure what they made, but it soon became clear it was bikes. That's how my connection with Honda started. Of course this was a time when even having a bicycle in Japan was something, and if you even sat on a motorbike you risked being told off. You had to have an interest in bikes to get into Honda. You have to remember that Mr Honda was the company president! Ordinary employees didn't get many chances to speak with him. However, a racing team was established and we developed and learnt the ropes racing in Japan. It was also declared that, come what may, we would, one day, go to the Isle of Man. I started racing at the Asama Kazan Races in 1955, on a 250cc machine. I must stress that at that time nearly

> all roads in Japan were gravel. This made conditions difficult, thundering along with stones flying everywhere and also damaging the bikes. Because of the gravel roads Honda had to build a two-kilometre straight track at Arakawa for us to test and practise on. I came off about three times, but always finished, sometimes with the bike over my shoulder! On one occasion I couldn't stop – and crashed into a post office. I managed to finish second in that race, and after it was over I went with Mr Honda to apologise to the boss of the post office. On subsequent occasions Mr Honda would visit the post office manager, but because Mr Honda's background was technical and the manager's clerical, conversation didn't flow easily. On these occasions the manager's wife would summon me as I could lighten the atmosphere. This helped me bond with Mr Honda. So, I went to Asama, crashed into the post office and through that got to know Mr Honda quite well … that's how it developed. But, every year it was, are we going … are we going … are we going? It took four years of preparation.[13]

Thus it was not 1955 when Honda returned to race on the Island, as they had initially promised, but 1959. The problems that they had faced were not only technical, but bureaucratic. Travel outside of Japan was still closely controlled at this time and Honda had difficulty in obtaining passports for this first trip. Neither civil servants nor politicians knew anything about international racing or of its potential importance to Japan. The firm got around this difficulty by the clever ruse of claiming that the team were temporary employees of an associated import company. For Taniguchi the memory of that journey, his first trip outside of Japan, remained strong for the rest of his life. There were no direct flights from Japan to

Europe at that time and the journey aboard a BOAC Comet took forty hours, stopping at Hong Kong, Rangoon, and Karachi along the way. He continues:

> It was only when on the first leg of the flight, to Hong Kong, that we actually believed it was happening. When we arrived the Honda people were told to stay on the plane while the rest of the passengers disembarked – we were puzzled and thought we must have done something wrong! It was because there was a large press contingent waiting. The reporters came on to the plane to ask some questions. The team from the Far East, from Japan had arrived! We knew little about the Island and they knew little about us. We had to struggle through this to the hotel. There were lots of questions – 'where did you buy the engine? Is it from Hong Kong?' They didn't seem to think we actually made such things in Japan! Remember, we had only gravel roads at that time … Japan only emerged as a modern country with the 1964 Olympics. Before that it was only outdoor toilets.[14]

Murray Walker was also there, and adds:

> When they had been over in 1954, they had been taking photographs of the works Norton, in particular the engine, the petrol tank, the rear suspension, the front suspension, the carburetor, you name it, and they said they were coming to race in the 125 class. The Japanese in those days had a reputation as very good copyists, so we thought they'll be back with a Manx Norton with a 125c hole in the barrel. Well when they came back in 1959 with their 125 bikes, they were four-valve, double overhead

> camshaft, twin-cylinder, spring-framed, telescopic-forked devices that were light years ahead of anything that we had got in that class.[15]

Such was Honda's commitment to the venture that they sent five riders, Naomi Taniguchi, Giichi Suzuki, Teisuke Tanaka, Junzo Suzuki and Bill Hunt, a smaller number of mechanics, four practice motorcycles and five racing machines, as well as enough spares and tools to set up a self-contained workshop. The race team captain was the American Bill Hunt, who was employed by Honda's US arm. He had visited the Isle of Man earlier in the year in preparation for the arrival of the full team. On that occasion he had filmed each bend on the Mountain Course, to which the Japanese had given numbers instead of the usual names. The film had then been studied extensively in Japan before the team set off on their long flight from Tokyo to London. Further detail on Hunt's preparation was given in a somewhat sneering article by John Quirk in the *Isle of Man Daily Times*, which also reflected some of the prevailing attitudes of the day:

> … taking pictures of every corner along the 37¾ miles of road and numbering them in sequence … means there is no necessity for the riders to have the shattering experience of memorising Clookshank's, B'gallow, Qually Bends and Cleg-ny-Baa. They will know the course by Left 1, Right 2, Left 2, Right 3 and so on. Mind you, there's a good prospect of a hot paragraph if one rider forgets the sequence and finds himself in the river at Right 31 – or Sulby Bridge to you. It is interesting to know, however, that there is a race track attached to the Honda works, nearly a mile long, and one sharp corner bears the title of 'Ramsey Hairpin.' Apart from the corners the Nipponese

> team will be given an idea of the surface they may kiss should things go wrong. Mr Hunt placed a shilling on the roadway to give comparison with the tarred granite chippings used by the Highway Board, and this was photographed.
>
> If he was meticulous in taking back essential data to Tokyo Mr Hunt was equally exacting when fixing accommodation for the riders and mechanics who will arrive from Japan early in May. A provisional booking was made at the Nursery Hotel, Onchan …
>
> In the arrangements for feeding and sleeping … the Nursery licensees will have to re-orientate their catering ideas when their Oriental guests arrive. Arrangements are being made by Mr Hunt to bring over plenty of bamboo shoots and dried fish from Japan – the staple food of the Nipponese contingent. And no doubt there will be plenty of flied lice. Another unusual feature is that the Japanese people do not like furniture in their rooms, and they will certainly dispense with beds. Everyone in that far country is quite happy to have a mattress on the floor and nothing else.
>
> It is perhaps as well that the Isle of Man does not attract too many people from cherry blossom land – one wonders how the Tourist Board could apply their proposed regulations to rooms without furniture and mattresses without beds! At the same time an influx of Oriental customers could provide Manx agriculture with a new outlet – pre-packaged bamboo shoots. And what an ideal thing it would be to turn the Ballaugh Curraghs into paddy fields.[16]

However, there was one crucial error in the Japanese preparations, as Taniguchi remembered:

We certainly studied very hard before we went, we had English lessons, however you didn't hear much English spoken at that time in Japan. Certainly when we entered Honda we never thought we'd go overseas. To go to the Isle of Man was a dream, but we knew nothing about the place. Honda staff had been there, so we had maps and such like about the course, the 60km Mountain Circuit. However, when we got there we found we wouldn't be using it – instead we'd be riding the Clypse Course! Totally different! We went there straight away to start learning it. The locals would shout and wave at us, saying things like, 'This is not the course, go back and turn left …' Somehow, despite such misunderstandings, we mastered the course. When we got to the Isle of Man a lot of our stuff was still en route, sent by ship via the Indian Ocean, all the machines, the test bikes and the race bikes. When we got the machines they'd been attacked by rust, on the brakes and elsewhere, causing serious problems, so we had to work really hard to prepare them for racing. All our other equipment, racing suits, helmets etc, was also in the container – a two-month voyage. When we tried to ride the course, the chains were a problem and stretched, the plugs were totally useless and the tyres lost their tread. We had to use local Renold chains and Avon tyres. Our main goal was not to damage the machines. Indeed, Mr Honda specifically told us, 'This is your first attempt, just don't break things, just make it to the finish. Don't crash. You don't need to worry about a result. You will have another chance!'

But the difference between the other factory riders and Honda's riders was that we were all able to prepare and maintain our own bikes. Because of that we had the advantage of knowing our bikes, knowing not to stress the engine and cause jumping valves, piston 'touch', valve dropping etc. So these things didn't happen to us. We knew all the parts of the engine. That was the advantage the Honda team had.[17]

The practise machines were of the Honda Benly model, a street bike first produced in 1953, which had a four-stroke 125cc engine of parallel twin configuration. The Benlys were easily identifiable by their sturdy pressed steel front forks, square-dialed speedometer, rectangular headlamp and boxy fuel tank. It was on these models that the Honda racers learned the intricacies of the Clypse Course on which they would actually be competing.

The race machines, designated RC142 by Honda were also of 125cc capacity, with a parallel twin configuration of 'over-square' dimensions; the engine/gear unit had a vertical shaft drive to the front overhead camshaft. Light alloy was used for all main castings and that included the cylinder heads, which were integral with each other. A heavily ribbed sump under the crank case carried 2 litres of oil. The crank case itself was also deeply finned and like that of the Benly was split horizontally rather than vertically, which was the case on British machines of the era. This simple innovation of turning the crank case split through 90 degrees had the effect of almost totally eliminating oil loss, a perennial problem with British machines. The RC142 also had an open spine frame, in which the engine was a stress bearing part, with leading link front and swing arm rear suspension.

The Honda team manager in 1959 was Yoshitaka Iida. His memory of the accommodation used by the squad differed in some details from the predictions of Mr Quirk:

We stayed at an inexpensive lodging called the Nursery Hotel and we even cut our own hair, but at least we did

> have regular meals. You can't go into battle on an empty stomach. Before we left, the Old Man told us, 'You're going as representatives of Japan, so don't embarrass us,' and he made us study table manners. So we ate bad food with good manners! The meat was always mutton. We'd use hand gestures to ask the waitress what the meat was, and the answer was inevitably, 'Baa.'[18]

Taniguchi recalled other aspects of the Nursery Hotel, and that it proved to be an education in more ways than one!

> We hadn't travelled before, so we thought it a fine hotel. However, the facilities, bathrooms and toilets, were limited. There was just one of each on both floors! We were based on the second floor, and therefore each day had to work out a rota to use the bath. Yet the biggest difficulty was the toilets! At that time in Japan there was little modern plumbing. We had never learnt to use a flush toilet. We had a rider Bill Hunt with us as a translator and he was a help regarding this, but if you didn't flush immediately the place filled up with smells, and we learnt to flush while actually doing a number two! We were always learning something new … I think even today some Japanese don't know how to flush properly … The things we learnt![19]

Fortunately for the team, they were befriended by the only Japanese person then resident on the Isle of Man, Mrs Keiko ('Kay') Carran, who had married a Manx serviceman stationed in Japan in the post-war years. She brought them Japanese foods such as rice cakes and sometimes acted as an interpreter. Mrs Carran remembered that when she learned the team were coming, she was eager to meet them as it was the first opportunity that she had had to speak her language in several years. In later decades she was honoured by the Honda company for the informal support that she had provided in these crucial years. Taniguchi remembered:

> There was a Japanese woman called Keiko San who lived on the Island and she taught us a fair bit about the place. As for the food, it seemed to be lamb every day! When we asked what the meal was we received a 'baaa' reply! On top of that we had no rice. These days there is a Japanese restaurant in the Isle of Man, but in those days nothing of the sort. Living for a month, eating mainly meat, and no rice, was enough to drive us crazy. However, Keiko San made us nigiri (rice balls), telling us to eat them and they would make us strong racers. It wasn't Japanese rice. (We had packed rice, and soy sauce and miso along with other food in the container which was sent from Japan, however, when it arrived it was all spoilt.) The food Keiko San prepared was fabulous, large portions as well. It set us up for the racing and I will certainly never forget it![20]

Another rider in the 1959 Honda team was Teisuke Tanaka. Like Taniguchi he had never before raced on a tarmac or paved road, only the gravel surfaces of the Japanese national highways or the Asama dirt track. He also remembered the team's arrival in the Isle of Man and their preparations:

> When we got to the Isle of Man and saw how different the conditions there were from Japan, I felt like shivering. There were sidewalks and stone walls on both sides of the road, and there was a semicylindrical ridge down the centre. So this public road is where we ride the Isle of Man TT Race, I thought. We've finally made it all the

> way here. The only thing left now is to go ahead on sheer determination. That was my first reaction. I rode around the course several times to memorise it, but it was such a difficult course that I almost panicked. I stopped along the way to take a break, and the islanders came up curiously to talk to me. 'Are you Japanese? Where is your motorcycle from?' I told them it was a Honda from Japan, but they seemed to have the idea that the Japanese weren't able to make motorcycles. They looked at my Benly very suspiciously.[21]

Honda Team Leader Kawashima remembered that they arrived a month ahead of time, so they were the first to show up on the Isle of Man. The other teams didn't arrive that early. Then he realised, almost as an afterthought, that of course the Isle of Man TT meeting wasn't the only event in the World Championship – there were other Grand Prix races. Shortly afterwards the others started to show up and begin training, and to his concern, they were very fast. For Kawashima racing at top level on the Isle of Man was a shock:

> The riders and the mechanics of other teams were on such a different level from us that at first I was seriously discouraged. I soon recovered, though. I started feeling very competitive, and I thought, all right, if we don't win this year, then just you wait until next year! All of us were eager to compete again the following year, including me. Whether you call it youth or stupidity, I don't know … There is something very distinctively Honda about this![22]

Shunji Hirota was a Honda mechanic in 1959. He remembered:

> When we got to the Isle of Man, things were just as they had been in Japan. All of us, from the team leader on down,

> worked till late. The way we saw it, it was easier working at night, when we didn't have spectators. Then it appeared in the newspaper that the Japanese were like mice in the attic. You could hear them scurrying around at night, it said.[23]

Newspapers also reported that the Japanese worked Saturdays and Sundays, too, so their performance must be low. However, the Honda mechanics faced an uphill challenge to get their machines ready in time. Everyone from riders to team manager pitched in to help. The first thing to do was clean the rust off the machines when they were unpacked after the long sea journey from Japan.

The four-valve cylinder heads, which had not been ready in time to be sent by ship, arrived by air freight. Only three of the machines would have their cylinder heads replaced in time for racing. The Benly engine was running very well. However, until better-quality replacements could be sourced the tyres, which wore out, and the chains, which soon stretched, had to be replaced daily. The spark plugs lost their electrodes, holes opened up in the pistons, and the team found out beyond any doubt that some of the made-in-Japan parts were still far from world class. The helmets they had brought from Japan failed to pass the Auto Cycle Union scrutineers' inspection, so they were directed to use Cromwell helmets, made in England, which they bought locally.

The engine aside, the bottom-link front suspension looked out of date and there were concerns about both frame rigidity and brake performance. Honda's test course, built along the Arakawa River, was a simple arrangement of two flat, straight runs. The data from testing there simply was not relevant to the Clypse course, which had many ascending and descending slopes and seventy-four different curves.

Quite apart from the racing preparations, there was a unique cultural dimension to the arrival of the Honda team at the 1959 TT, and their presence on the Isle of Man that year (and subsequently) did much to rebuild Anglo-Japanese relations, which had been badly damaged by the war. The young Japanese riders experienced a culture shock on arriving for the first time in a western country, but equally for young Manx lads, whose only preconceptions about the Japanese were probably negative ones received from parents, it was an eye-opening situation. It would not be an exaggeration to say that the Japanese were hated by many British people who had lived through and fought in the Second World War, but here was perhaps the first post-war generation unburdened by those emotions. Among them was Roy Moore, a youngster living in Onchan in 1959. He remembered the Honda team at the Nursery Hotel:

> While Onchan School taught many things it did not include Japan or Japanese culture on the agenda for 11/12 year olds, so when it was revealed that four Japanese riders plus mechanics would be in our presence for the TT races at the Nursery we didn't really know what to expect. It must have been put to them that this was a public relations exercise as well as a learning curve for Honda motorcycles. Nothing was refused and many were the hats, badges and various advertising literature and goods dispensed with a smile by the very friendly bunch. For many years as well as my silver Honda badge (still in my possession) I had a tin of rice with a Japanese label.
>
> Round and round the Clypse Course went the group on their Benlys with the riders picking up a little English by saying 'Race bikes arrive soon' … [as] I was having tea in

> the Cannell household at 69 Nursery Avenue at about 6pm prior to practice week the sound of an open megaphone machine indicated to us that the race bikes had arrived! Within a minute we were out into the back lane and over the fence to the long driveway which formed the lower entrance to the Nursery Hotel.
>
> This entrance was never used – the big white gates being shut and all visitors used the top entrance … the surface therefore was suspect with moss, bird droppings and other things which didn't afford much grip! It was either Honda No 3 or No 4 being bump started by the mechanics which produced a unique happening – the first crash of a Honda on the Isle of Man! When the engine cranked into life the man at the controls whipped out the clutch and applied the front brake … with the drive conditions the others must have struck lucky and got some grip. Unfortunately this one didn't and with Geoff and myself watching and the two mechanics finding everything quite amusing the unfaired machine was laid on its side![24]

Another Onchan resident, the Isle of Man's former Minister for Home Affairs and stalwart TT supporter Adrian Earnshaw, remembered the arrival of the Honda team in the village in 1959:

> A 'buzz' of excitement went round the Village when it was learned Honda had decided to base their team at the Nursery Hotel. Youngsters like me, unused to seeing people of foreign nationalities, were totally curious and fascinated by the sight of Japanese mechanics and competitors landing in 'planet Onchan'! This was heightened when word got round that the bikes and

riders were pretty good. Also they were handing out loads of 'goodies', manna from heaven for young boys like me consumed by TT enthusiasm.

Such was the excitement generated by the team's presence, that each afternoon of practice week, as soon as the school bell rang, there would be a charge up the lane to be first arrival at the Nursery. The machines were housed at the rear of the hotel yard. Work on the bikes was conducted outdoors in the yard. None of us were permitted into the yard but could view the activity from the pillared gateway. The competition to be at the front when the badges and other freebies were handed out created quite a frenzy with children clambering up the backs of each other to occupy the front row.

My memories were of the good organisation of the team, the oil-free cleanliness of the machines and the matching slatey-grey overalls of the mechanics. The Nursery Hotel remained Honda's base for (I think) three formative years.[25]

In a report on Practice Week results, the *Isle of Man Daily Times* observed that:

The practice performances of the riders have not been the cause of any sensation and the fastest of the Nippon riders, Naomi Taniguchi, has been a minute slower than the fastest man in the preliminaries. But there is a strong suspicion that the head of the menage, American Bill Hunt, has been 'foxing' during the past week and that the Japanese trio. J. Suzuki, G. Suzuki and Taniguchi have been riding to a set schedule – giving nothing away. Nothing has been left undone to have the machines at peak performance for tomorrow's event. Ever since

> practising finished on Friday morning intensive work has been going on in the portable garage set up at the Nursery Hotel at Onchan.[26]

When the 125cc Ultra-Lightweight event got under way, as expected the race was dominated by MZ and MV Agusta. However, four of the five Honda riders finished, with only Bill Hunt retiring after he came off at Ballacoar in the second lap, although he was unhurt. Taniguchi put in the strongest performance, finishing sixth. He was followed by Giichi Suzuki in seventh and Teisuke Tanaka in eighth. Junzo Suzuki finished in eleventh place. This resulted in the award of the Team Prize to the Honda squad, a remarkable achievement at their first attempt. Honda employees' spirits rose as a result. They truly felt that they had come close to the world's top class. Taniguchi recalled the jubilant welcome that the team received upon returning home:

> It was tremendous! Mr Honda, Mr Fujisawa, various bigwigs, plenty of others and the press, were waiting at Haneda airport. Everyone was celebrating! Above everything, even the achievements, Mr Honda was most happy that we had arrived back safe and sound. I'll never forget the look on the boss's face![27]

Team manager Yoshitaka Iida remembered:

> A special edition of the Honda Company News had the president's remarks: 'I am extremely happy that we were able to achieve results like this. The team leader, the riders, and the mechanics all did splendidly. I want to thank all of you who created these machines. However, we still have to deal with the matter of first through fifth place.' These are

> great lines that you'd only hear from the Old Man. I loved them because they expressed exactly what he was feeling.[28]

If the Japanese had encountered some prejudice or even hostility from the motorcycle racing establishment on their first arrival on the Isle of Man in 1954, then this was in complete contrast to impressions of them by the time they left in 1959. In a glowing editorial in *Motor Cycling*, R.R. Holliday wrote:

> So the Japanese T.T. equipe did not have their long, long trek for nothing! After exhibiting a thoroughness in preparation and a diligence in course-learning and practice that was an object lesson to many of the older hands, their skill, courage and road craft on race day and the speed of their machines was among the factors which gave colour to the smallest, but most exciting event of T.T. Week.
>
> It is to be hoped that the 125cc team prize, which they will carry back to Tokyo, will spur Hondas to even greater efforts in the future so that the mutually beneficial bounds of motorcycling sport, which knows no discrimination of race or creed, will be spread even wider.[29]

However, few people now remember that one member of the Honda team never made it to the Isle of Man in 1959. His name was Kunihiko Akiyama. He had practised at Asama with the other members of the team but tragically lost his life while filming a motorcycle stunt in April 1959, just one month before the firm made its debut at the TT. Taniguchi remembered that of all of them, Akiyama had the most ambition and greatest dreams for the Isle of Man. He also stressed what an accomplished individual he was: a graduate from Nihon University, fluent in English, skilled in judo and kendo, he was the keenest of the trainee Honda riders.

He was laid to rest at the historic shrine of Gotokuji to the west of Tokyo, and today a bronze statue of a rider clad in 1950s leathers, goggles and helmet stands upon his grave, making it easy to identify amid the headstones. The rider's hand is raised in salute to the teammates who went on to make motorcycle history, and the statue is orientated so that he looks forever over the horizon, toward the Isle of Man. In the midst of the Japanese katakana inscription on his headstone the letters TT can be clearly identified. The full translation reads:

> This is a statue of Mr Kunihiko Akiyama who died by an unexpected accident during a film shooting of a race scene. He was 24 when he died; he was going to participate in the Tourist Trophy race in the Isle of Man in 1959. That Tourist Trophy race was the number one motorcycle race in the world. He couldn't realise his aim to participate in the TT race. He was very enthusiastic about this, however his dream about the TT race could not be realised … This statue was erected with the wish that he will look far west to the Isle of Man forever, with this hope that he had in his younger days for his life.[30]

That, however, was not his only memorial, for as Taniguchi remembered:

> On the way to the airport at Haneda we stopped at Mr Akiyama's home. His father gave us a lock of his son's hair and requested we take it to the Isle of Man; we buried the lock of hair at Ballacarrooin Hill, a small hill at the Clypse circuit, so that every time we passed it he would be an inspiration to us and his spirit would be

> with us. I also kept a small photo of the deceased close to my chest.[31]

So it was that from these humble beginnings sprang the international fame that Honda would eventually enjoy. Soichiro Honda never forgot the importance of this small island in launching his company on to the world stage. In the words of Taniguchi:

> I'd like the people of the Isle of Man to know that to Mr Honda, the Island was a special place, and he was devoted to it more than anywhere else.[32]

Chapter Two

1960–61

HONDA, HONDA, HONDA ALL THE WAY

Although the Honda squad had carried off the team prize at the TT in 1959 (a creditable achievement) their riders at that time were inexperienced in racing on the Isle of Man. Soichiro Honda himself recognised that there was still some way to go, both in terms of machinery and riders, before they would achieve individual success. He knew he could improve on the speed and performance of his bikes through hard work, but recognised that Honda would also need to recruit western riders with TT experience if they were to gain podium places. He also freely acknowledged another reason why foreign riders were crucial to the development of the company. Due to the prevailing cultural norms in Japan at that time, their own riders were often extremely reluctant to criticise the motorcycle, to the point that they would continue to ride a machine that was obviously broken, rather than suffer what they saw as the embarrassment of personal conflict over it. Foreign riders had no such qualms about telling a mechanic or team boss exactly what was wrong with a machine, or how it could be improved.

In 1960 on the Isle of Man the firm competed in both the 125cc Ultra-Lightweight TT and 250cc Lightweight event, the latter using a four-stroke, four-cylinder machine, the RC161, which aroused great interest on the Island. The engine was basically two 125cc units mounted together as a square four, with double overhead camshafts. The cylinders were inclined at 35 degrees to increase airflow over them and thereby improve cooling. The engine blocks were cast in one piece along with the top part of the horizontally split crankcases, which were made of light alloy. This was to stiffen the engine; when cylinder case and crankcase are separate, the crank has a natural tendency to make the two flex and scrub against each other at the join, thereby destroying any gasket or seal between them. The cylinder heads were also of light alloy (cast in one piece for the four cylinders). The various covers were cast in electron, an alloy of aluminium and magnesium. The double overhead camshafts were now driven from the centre of the crankshaft by a gear train between the cylinders. To reduce the width of the engine, this gear train was partially situated behind the cylinders, and from there drove the magneto for the ignition.

It produced 38bhp at the rear wheel at 14,000 rpm; the tyres were a quarter inch bigger than those on the 125 at 2.75in front and 3.00in rear, and the petrol tank was nearly twice as big at 5½ gallons, while the oil tank held ⅔ gallon. Like the 125 it had a six-speed gearbox, and also like the 125 its maximum speed (130.49mph) was achieved in fifth gear. This fact piqued the curiosity of racing journalist Geoff Davison, who wrote to the Honda Motor Company about it. His reply, received by return of post, stated:

> As to the maximum speed of RC143 and RC161, we could only use 5th gear owing to the fact that there was not a suitable course in Japan.[1]

This he took to mean that there were no roads in Japan suitable for top-gear performance, which of course in turn meant that the machines might well be capable of even greater speeds. In the 125cc class the RC143 was a completely different bike from the previous year's RC 142, the most conspicuous change being the switch from leading link front suspension to telescopic front forks, and although the frame was still of the spine type, practically everything else on the cycle was new. The brakes were changed from single-sided two leading shoes to double-sided single leading shoe. The drive to the camshafts was still by means of bevel shaft and gears, but the cylinders were now inclined under 35 degrees. The position of the magneto was changed from the inlet camshaft to a place behind the cylinders. Bore and stroke were still 44 × 41 mm, and the power output was now 23bhp at 14,000 rpm. The carburetors still had remote float bowls, and the dry weight was 93kg.

For the Japanese riders in the squad, this would be their first time riding on the Mountain Circuit, as the Clypse Course had now been abandoned, and all races would now take place on the big course. Six Honda machines started the opening 125cc races, with five ridden by Japanese competitors and one by Australian Tom Phillis, who was entered by the firm before the meeting. He had first approached Honda to offer his services as a rider in 1959, before anyone else had even begun to think of taking them seriously. Born in Sydney, Tom had started his career as an apprentice motorcycle mechanic, before breaking into the racing scene in his native Australia. In the early days people frequently misquoted his name, calling him Phillips instead of Phillis, which greatly annoyed him. He told his parents that he was intending to change his name by deed poll, but his father countered with 'Don't change it son. Make it famous.' That was exactly what he did and in 1958 he and his wife sold everything in order to move to Europe so that he could break into the Grand Prix scene. On the second lap of the race Phillis, who was holding fifth place, lost time when he pulled into the pits to change a misfiring plug. His teammate Moto Kitano meanwhile frightened the spectators at Keppel Gate by opening up too fiercely as he came out of the corner, getting into a tail-wagging slide in the process, but he managed to stay aboard. Taniguchi was the first Honda rider home, in sixth place, and just as it looked as if all of the Honda machines would make it back intact, word came in to the effect that Kitano was touring at the Guthrie Memorial having suffered mechanical trouble. The Roads Open car followed him back to the pits.

The Lightweight Race followed, and this time there would be two Australian riders as part of the Honda squad, with Phillis joined by Bob Brown, who took over the 250cc mount that Tanaka had been nominated to ride, after the Japanese rider crashed and was injured during Practice Week. The firm had first approached John Hartle to ride it, and though this came to nothing, he did ride for Honda later in the year at the Dutch TT. Brown placed fourth in the Lightweight, and Phillis had been in third before retiring, having struggled in practice as the gear change and rear brake levers were reversed. Giichi Suzuki retired at Quarter Bridge on the third lap due to a gearbox failure, but Kitano finished in fifth place, which was enough to secure him the Overseas Newcomers' Trophy for best performance by a non-winner. Bob Brown, like Phillis, was also from Sydney, and might well have had a longer career in the Honda team were it not for the fact that he was sadly killed a month later while racing in West Germany. Both Lightweight races, however, were dominated by MV Agusta.

Overall there was a greater profusion of works machines than had been seen on the Island for some years, yet it was telling that there was not a single entry from a British factory, and the smaller classes were becoming a struggle between the thus far dominant Italian factories, and the up and coming Japanese firms. British concern Norton were still in contention for the Senior TT, and the following year would see them take victory in that class, but overall the writing was on the wall for United Kingdom factories. Unlike the British motorcycle industry, obliged to make the best of old designs, produced on old machinery, Honda operated in an upward-moving business climate in which profit could be reinvested in Research and Development, and the most advanced production equipment, rather than leaked away to impatient stockholders. Honda were thereby able to carry out the intensive research necessary for achieving success.

It was reported that the 1960 racing programme had cost Honda £450,000, which included the cost of designing, building and developing the 250cc four-cylinder model, and improving the 125cc twin. It also included the cost of flying riders, mechanics and bikes to Europe and back from Tokyo, and the cost of chartering planes to travel between European meetings. Shortly after the TT, Rhodesian rider Jim Redman had been recruited to the team, to replace the injured Tom Phillis. It was at the Dutch TT at Assen, shortly after its Isle of Man namesake that Phillis came off in practice and broke his collar bone. While visiting him in his caravan on the circuit, Redman mentioned the fact that he was keen to take over the Australian's 125cc machine, and Phillis offered to put in a good word for him with the team management. Redman was a tough character, hardened by his early experiences in life. Born in Hampstead, London, he and his two younger siblings had been orphaned shortly after the Second World War. At the age of just sixteen, he was earning what he could to keep the family together before deciding to emigrate to southern Africa in search of work. He got a job with the government transport department in Bulawayo, but his heart was in motorcycle racing and after honing his skills for several years in the South African racing scene he came to Europe. Success had been slight, however, and by 1959 he was ready to give it all up to become a tobacco farmer. He gave himself just one more season to make it big in Europe. When Honda offered Jim the chance to ride their 125cc machine, his dream had come true:

> I couldn't believe my ears, at last the chance I had been waiting for so long. … Now I had this golden opportunity … I felt I would be able to give a good account of myself the next day on Honda's 125. I knew that I had my future in my hands: if I failed I would have only myself to blame.[2]

Honda did not expect too much from Redman at his first outing for them in Holland in 1960. After all, he was unfamiliar with the machine, having never ridden one before. In fact, he put in a better time than Phillis had managed. Race manager Kawashima was delighted, and his place in the team was assured. By September of that year, word had spread that he was hoping to ride a Honda in the late-season meetings and in the winter races in southern Africa. He remembered:

> The Japanese firm was the object of derision from some individuals in and around GP racing, who thought these little Japanese machines would never be a danger to the big teams of the time, the MVs and MZs. Even though they still needed to be improved, the results obtained … at the TT were very encouraging.[3]

Kiyoshi Kawashima was Honda team leader in 1959 and 1960. He noticed that now, things were changing and the Honda name was gaining respect. From the second year of competition onwards, things had changed completely, to the extent that it was like the difference between night and day. This was true both in Japan and in other countries. For one thing, they received travel permission from the Japanese government right away. At the London airport, the year before they had just been a group of suspicious people carrying motorcycle parts in their luggage. Now, though, customs officials recognised them, saying, 'Hey, Honda!' and just waved them through. The change in ordinary people's awareness of motor sports was also very apparent.

Early in 1961 Luigi Taveri, the diminutive German-speaking Swiss pilot with an Italian name, was considering quitting top-flight motorcycle racing. He had started his career as a sidecar passenger for his brother, but later switched to solos, and due to his slight stature became a specialist on the smaller machines. He had first appeared at the TT in 1955, riding for MV Agusta, but his best positions had been second places. As his relationship with MV had cooled, he had flirted with privately owned Ducatis and even the East German MZ firm. Reluctantly, now he had decided to hang up his helmet and boots. He takes up the story:

> The first World Championship round in Barcelona in 1961 had already been staged without my participation. But very soon I missed racing, I could hardly stand to ride without it. But my decision was made: I didn't want to compete anymore. My wife felt that I was not satisfied with myself because I was convinced that I could have done more. However, she did not talk to me about it, but wrote (without my knowledge) to the Honda works in Japan. Soon she received an answer: 'Your husband should contact our racing team. We are interested in the possibility of him riding for us.' Suddenly everyone else was forgotten! Of course I wanted to take this

opportunity. I immediately flew to Amsterdam, the seat of the Honda team. I had to conduct the meetings with team leader Kawashima. Kawashima looked like a school boy. I couldn't imagine that his word carried any weight in a large company like Honda. But at that time it did not occur to me that the Japanese should not be measured in any way by our standards. Kawashima was the head of the racing team, today, he holds the position of a director in the Honda Group and takes third place in the hierarchy of the management structure (Mister Honda personally heads it).

'If you had spoken to us earlier, it would have been possible for us to plan differently. Now our team is complete with Redman, Phillis, Tanaka, Taniguchi, Shimazaki and Kitano. But because we expect a lot from you, we can provide you with a model from last year. If you get good results with it, you will get a new machine after the third race. However, it is not possible for us to engage you permanently. We will pay you from race to race.'

With this, Kawashima presented me with the alternative of riding for Honda under not very good conditions, or retiring. I asked for time to think about it and drove home. Should I take the risk and commit myself to a brand again under unsatisfactory conditions? Wasn't it really time to give up racing? – But I was still too ambitious to retire and loved racing too much![4]

As a result, in 1961 at the Ultra-Lightweight TT the Honda factory team fielded three western riders, Phillis, Redman and Taveri. They also numbered two Japanese riders, Sadao Shimazaki and Naomi Taniguchi, while Moto Kitano and Teisuke Tanaka were not present. This time they were using the 2RC143, the improved version of the RC143. The spine frame of the latter had been abandoned to make way for an open, double-loop frame, with a tube arrangement around the steering head as in the Norton Featherbed frame. The engine, however, was more or less identical with that of the previous year. Jim Redman gave his views on the machines to Graham Walker:

> I'm very pleased with them, they're going very well indeed; I had a bit of trouble with the 125 in practice but we've been up on the Mountain this morning. It's pretty cool up there. The 250 cc revs at 13,500, the smaller machine is the same, it's the same engine really with only the centre two pots.[5]

Honda machinery had quickly demonstrated to other riders just how good it was. One of these riders was the young Mike Hailwood, aged just twenty-one when he came to the 1961 TT. A public school-educated son of a millionaire, he was anything but the typical image of a motorcycle racer. Even his rivals were forced to admit after racing against him a few times that, whatever his father's money had bought him, it was not the innate natural skill that he had on a motorbike. If he was young, however, he was far from inexperienced. Hailwood was seventeen when he began motorcycle racing and his wealthy father Stan, the owner of King's of Oxford, paid for him to go to South Africa to practise and hone his skills under the tuition of more experienced riders. He rode in his first TT in 1958, and three years later had seen the way in which Honda machinery was developing, as well as its potential.

It was as a privateer in his father's Ecurie Sportive team that Hailwood entered his 125cc Honda in the Ultra-Lightweight race that year, although he did receive some factory assistance. Honda differed from other manufacturers at this time in as much as the racing bikes that they supplied to privateers and satellite teams were every bit as good as those used by their own factory team. Soichiro Honda believed that a win was a win whoever rode the bike, so long as it had his name on the side. However, Hailwood was almost a non-starter because the bike that his father had ordered from Honda nearly didn't turn up. Mike himself was quite resigned to the fact, but his father was more determined, and pestered the Honda team constantly. Stan tells us:

> Honda had promised Mike both a 125 and a 250, but there was a shortage of 125s and not until the final practice session, after persistent worrying, did we get a 125. I practically lived at the Honda camp that day and in the end, just to get rid of me I think, they said: 'All we have is Taveri's practice machine.' They told me it was a bit worse for wear but I could take it. Naturally I grabbed it and had it back at our camp before they could change their minds. We looked it over and Mike took it up the road. His remarks are perhaps, better left unsaid. In short, it was 'clapped out'. However, we decided he should do one lap very gently to get used to it and comply with the regulations. He came in and told me he was staggered by the performance and only wished it was in better shape. We went over everything, checking nuts, bolts, etc but without much hope of it lasting the course.[6]

Mike later recalled that his mechanics tightened up just about anything they could lay a spanner on as they prepared the machine, and this did have the effect of smoothing it out a little. Even so, he and his father had little confidence that the 125 would go the distance. The Ultra-Lightweight 125cc race was scheduled for the morning of Monday, 12 June 1961, with Honda factory rider Jim Redman leading the field away. After half a lap, Taveri and Hailwood had caught Redman, passing him before the Guthrie Memorial. As the two diced for first place, Hailwood broke the lap record by 2mph. This incredibly exciting event was captured on one of the earliest pieces of colour film shot at the TT, with commentary by Graham Walker, who utters the memorable line, 'It's Honda, Honda, Honda all the way' as the top three positions were held by the trio of Taveri, Hailwood and Tom Phillis all jostling for position. Taveri describes the importance of the race to him, after a couple of previous outings in Honda colours:

> … the team management was satisfied with me, because I received a new Honda machine for the Tourist Trophy, i.e. a race earlier than agreed. Now I had to prove my skills to secure a permanent place in the Japanese team. And I wanted to get wins! I set the fastest time in practice. This time I had some hopes to finally win a TT race, but now Mike Hailwood was also riding a Honda. I was assigned the start number five, he was number seven. So far, odd numbers had usually not brought me luck. But it was really not the time to be superstitious.
>
> An actual disadvantage, on the other hand, was that Hailwood would start the race ten seconds behind me. So I had to go away fast from the start. But in the second of the three laps, Hailwood had caught up with me. I tried everything to break away from him again, but it is not a little thing to get away from Mike Hailwood, the most successful and maybe best racing driver of all time! I had

one advantage: I am lighter than Hailwood. So my chance was on the upward slope after passing through the town of Ramsey. On this small mountain pass I was actually able to gain some distance from him.

Afterwards I looked back several times, but I couldn't see any sign of Hailwood. When I crossed the finish line, I started counting the seconds. About ten seconds after me, Hailwood flew over the line.

My British rival and I awaited the report of the loud speaker with the greatest tension. He had beaten me by two seconds. But I had proven to Kawashima (and myself) what I was capable of. I also had the certainty of being in a good racing team and to be able to ride under the same conditions as the others. With the third place of Tom Phillis and the fourth of Jim Redman, Honda's triumph was complete.[7]

Stan Hailwood was at the Grandstand, and recounts the excitement of the duel:

It was agreed that Mike should go flat out until it packed up. We were staggered when, on the first lap, he caught Honda's lightweight star Luigi Taveri, who had started ten seconds earlier, to smash the lap record from a standing start. On the second lap he broke it again, setting a new record, and increasing his lead over Taveri. Came the last lap and going up the Mountain the expected happened. The edge went off the motor and Taveri, two stones lighter, began catching up. Mike went berserk on corners trying to keep up but Luigi pulled away on the straights. We were sweating in the pits as Taveri came in first, and counting the seconds for Mike to arrive. He only just managed to win … A close shave![8]

Not only was this Mike's first ever TT win, but also the first for Honda. However grateful Honda might have been to the Hailwood family for delivering this, they did not allow it to intrude into business affairs, and still billed Mike's father Stan for £200 for shipping the bike! The machine on which he won was designated as a 2RC143 by the factory that built it. It was an improvement on the previous year's RC143, and this in turn was an improvement on the preceding RC142. In contrast to the RC142, the air-cooled, four-stroke, twin-cylinder engine of the RC143 was canted forward by 35 degrees to improve cooling and increase air flow to the newly designed Kei-hin carburetors. The engine featured double overhead camshafts, driven by a vertical shaft through bevel gears. The engine was said to produce 22bhp (16kW) at 14,000 rpm. The leading link front forks, which had proved successful on Japanese dirt tracks, had been identified as a particular weakness on tarmac and were replaced by more conventional telescopic forks for the Isle of Man. This change to the forks, along with the change to the engine design, helped move the centre of gravity of the bike much further forward. The open-cradle frame was also considerably strengthened as against the previous year's model. Hailwood wrote of it:

> I have already given my impression of the Honda 125 c.c. twin and there is little I can add except to say it is, without doubt, the finest 125 I have ever ridden. Although it is not nearly as outstanding in its class as the 250 c.c. Honda four, it is nevertheless a superb machine which combines ample, smooth power with perfect handling.[9]

The 1961 Ultra-Lightweight also saw the first non-works entry of a Honda in a TT race. Bob Rowe from Kent used a privately owned CB92 Benley road bike, which he had purchased from a dealer, before altering the riding position, removing the electric starter to save weight and fitting a fairing.

The 1961 2RC143 gave both Honda and Hailwood their first win on the Isle of Man. At the time of course, Hailwood if not exactly an unknown was still a novice, so all of the media attention was focussed upon Honda. It is only in retrospect that it came to be seen as the first of a phenomenal series of wins by the legendary 'Mike the Bike'. It was also indicative of the strength of Honda technology that a machine that had taken such a battering during practice could subsequently turn in a race-winning performance. However some doubt exists as to what became of the actual motorcycle that Mike rode on that day in 1961. Some believe that the bike was subsequently presented by Soichiro Honda 'to the people of the Isle of Man', in grateful recognition of the part the Island had played in securing the future of his company, and that it resided for many years in the private Murray Motorcycle Museum on the Island. However, in the early 2000s the owner downsized, and sold this machine back to the Honda corporation. The Murray Museum website now states:

> One of the motorcycles that proved to be the most sought after, on display and for sale, was a Honda works 125cc twin cylinder, the racer from 1961. This was the bike that was given to Charlie [Murray] for [sic] Mr. Honda's private collection. In the mid-1970s, Mr Honda was on a world tour and made a visit to 'Murray's', whilst on the Isle of Man. Charlie asked Mr Honda through an interpreter, if it would be possible to have a Honda race motorcycle for the museum. When he returned home to Japan, he sent the 125cc racer as a gift. During the sale [of] the motorcycles in 2006, Peter [Murray] got in touch with Honda, and they informed him that they would like to

> 'buy' back the bike, so a price was agreed on and the bike went back to Honda Japan. As this motorcycle had come from Mr Honda's private collection, Honda were keen to have it back whatever the cost. The motorcycle was probably the race bike Kunimitsu Takahashi rode when he won the 1961 Ulster Grand Prix, and not the bike that Mike Hailwood rode when he won the 1961 T.T.[10]

Be that as it may, the Honda company apparently believed it to be the Hailwood machine, and the statement above also begs the question as to why the president of Honda would present the people of the Isle of Man with a machine that had won in Ireland! In any event, it now resides in the Honda Collection Hall at Hamamatsu, unequivocally labelled as the first Honda winner at the Isle of Man TT, ridden by Mike Hailwood. One other intriguing snippet of information also offers a clue as to the real fate of the Hailwood machine. As stated earlier, Honda billed Stan for £200 for the shipping of two machines from Japan (not for their purchase). This suggests that the machines were only on loan, a situation confirmed by the fact that Mike states in the book *Hailwood* (written by his friend Ted Macauley) that through a fiddle his father managed to hang on to the 250 machine, whereas letting the 125 go was no great loss, because he had decided to give up racing in that class as he was too heavy. This does imply that the 125 machine was returned to Honda, which further supports the theory that this after all was the true identity of the machine in the Murray museum; indeed both identities could be true – the Takahashi bike used at the Ulster Grand Prix in August could in theory be that previously used by Mike on the Island in June.

In the Lightweight 250cc race on the afternoon of 12 June 1961 there were two Japanese competitors (Kunimitsu Takahashi and Naomi Taniguchi) and three western riders (Redman,

Phillis and Bob McIntyre) under the official Honda banner, with Hailwood's Ecurie Sportive again as a Honda satellite team. Hailwood explained before the race that the machine was more or less his to do with as he wished:

> It was very decent of them, they lent it to us, and we're allowed to do anything we want to it within reason. We've done little things here and there which have helped a little bit, which I don't think they are allowed to do.[11]

Phillis also had some interesting comparisons to make between the 1961 machine and the previous year's model, when interviewed before the race:

> The new one is better, although having ridden the old one I've got quite used to that and I'm not anymore at home on the new one than I am on the older model. The new one is faster, and braking has improved but it has to be improved with the extra speed. Some of the extra speed comes from the streamlining as much as anything, that's been improved quite a lot. We normally race at about 13,500 revs; I don't exactly know the maximum speed, it's not a big concern of mine![12]

There was another Honda machine entered privately in this race, that of Fred Stevens, who was using a converted sports roadster rather that a true racing machine. However, it is a matter of TT trivia that he had the first electric starter to be used on the Island, and when the time keeper's flag dropped he simply pressed the button and sped off down Glencrutchery Road, with his starting companion still pushing! Scottish rider Bob McIntyre hailed from Glasgow, and had spent his early working life in the city's famous shipyards while he was beginning to break into motorcycling. He had entered TT folklore in 1957 when, riding for Gilera, he had set the first 100mph lap around the Mountain Course. McIntyre had first come into contact with Honda in their debut year at the TT, when he had been asked to go to the Nursery Hotel to write a newspaper article. He had the opportunity on that occasion to test ride a 125cc motorcycle, and to his amazement discovered it had the performance normally associated with a 350cc machine. In 1961 he had been offered a Honda ride via Reg Armstrong, the Honda agent in Dublin. Even though he was not a full member of the team, this was virtually a works machine and had been prepared by the factory mechanics. McIntyre wrote afterwards:

> I had never ridden in the Lightweight class before. I had always been interested only in the bigger machines and at 11½ stone I regard myself as a bit heavy even for a 250cc machine. But the Honda is a big 250 – more like a 500. I took up the offer with pleasure … in its classes the Honda is unbeatable but the handling could be improved.[13]

McIntyre had a lot on his plate at the 1961 TT because in addition to his Honda, he was due to ride a Bianchi twin in the Junior race and a single-cylinder Norton in the Senior. He notes:

> They all probably brake in the same amount of distance, but the difference of single to twin to four cylinder is a bit frightening, when it comes to the rev band you're inclined to forget for a moment which machine you're on. The controls are all the same, but people reckon that riding a four cylinder is more difficult in the wet, but I should say no, it's easier in the wet.[14]

McIntyre screamed away from the start line and dominated the first lap. As he flashed past the Grandstand for the first time it was announced that he had set a new lap record from a standing start. However the Flying Scotsman had even more amazing tricks up his sleeve for the second lap. This time around he posted a speed of 99.58mph, which beat the existing 350cc record. As MV rider Gary Hocking dropped out of contention it became a duel between McIntyre and Hailwood, with Phillis occupying third place by the third lap. By the fourth circuit, with a lighter tank there was now much debate among spectators and commentators as to whether McIntyre would go for the ton. One observer at Kepple Gate definitely thought that he was going faster now than on his previous three laps. On the fifth lap, however, he was seen to give a thumbs down as he passed the pits, and by the time the Sulby commentator noticed he was late, the reason became clear. McIntyre takes up the story once again:

> People were speculating, I heard later, on whether I would be the first to break the 'ton' barrier on a 250cc model. I could, in fact, have gone faster but my bike had given a warning slide on a left-hand bend and, when I glanced down, I saw oil on the tyre. My machine had suffered a mysterious oil leak from the engine throughout practice and we had been unable to cure it. With oil on the tyre I had to be careful. I slowed to 99.26 mph. My race average was now 99.23 mph.
>
> The engine was still running well as I came on to the last lap. Spectators were waving me on. Mike Hailwood, lying second to me, was half a minute behind. Then, at Quarry Bends, before Sulby Straight, my engine seized due to the loss of oil. I was prepared for this and was able to whip in the clutch immediately, but I was out of the race.[15]

The retirement of McIntyre through engine failure left the hard-pushing Hailwood to take the win, his second in one day. The final leader board showed Hondas in the five top places, with Hailwood, Phillis and Redman on the podium. The Honda 'A' team of Redman, Takahashi and Taniguchi won the 250cc Manufacturers' Team Award. This, however, belies the fact that the race was one of the greatest performances of Bob McIntyre's career. Hailwood later wrote of his 250cc model, which he called a 'non-works works bike':

> This, like the 125, is a magnificent machine. When riding close to a Honda four its handling looks frightful, but its looks belie it, for it feels perfectly all right and does not seem at all skittish. I never fell off a 250 Honda in spite of some hair-raising battles with riders of the calibre of Bob McIntyre, Tom Phillis, John Hartle, Kunimitsu Takahashi and Jim Redman, so its handling must be all right.[16]

Describing the race, he stated:

> [Gary Hocking and I] had quite a dice for the first lap, passing and re-passing and I think that went on into the second lap then he conked out with some obscure trouble which left me in second place behind Bob Mac. I was all on my own then, Tom Phillis was a little bit behind, and then on the last lap I saw Mac sitting by the side of the road along the Sulby Straight and I knew that if I didn't have any trouble I had it in the bag then.[17]

He added later:

> I had a lot of luck [in that race], I'll be the first to admit it, but I had to put in some damned hard riding as well.

> I suppose that many people would point out that if the leader hadn't been forced out in the 250 [race] I wouldn't have won … And that's true to a certain extent; but the main thing is that I had to be thereabouts when it happened and ready to take my chances. Luck is part of the game – after all, I had my share of bad fortune.[18]

Having just turned twenty-one that year, he continued:

> After the [1961] TT I felt that I'd really arrived as a motorcycle-racer. Successes on short circuits were all well and good, but a TT win had been my ambition from the start; it was, and still is, the severest test possible for both man and machine. I came of age on the island in more ways than one.[19]

In the 1961 250cc RC162, the spine frame had also been replaced, as per the 125 model, and the new frame was also of the open, double-loop type. The frame tubes did not have the same diameter everywhere; where they joined the steering head, they tapered out to a larger diameter for increased strength and rigidity. Unlike in its predecessor the RC161, the engine cylinders were now inclined at 30 degrees, and the engine was 80mm narrower to improve aerodynamics; it also no longer had a wet sump – that of the RC161 had sat between the exhaust pipes, which had hindered oil cooling despite the fins on the sump. The oil was now carried in a tank under the seat. This latter move, however, was in the first instance not a great success, as the bikes still suffered from overheating; indeed Honda wrestled with this problem for a long time. The result of small cylinder size and large piston crown and combustion chamber surface area was very hot-running engines, which ran into lubrication trouble as hot oil lost viscosity – or even boiled. Honda struggled to overcome this, carrying the oil alternately in a finned sump (as on the Italian fours) or in a remote tank (British and German practice), and finally adopting oil coolers from aviation practice.

The 250cc machine that Mike used that day was later presented by Soichiro Honda to the National Motor Museum at Beaulieu, in the New Forest. It features a cross-over linkage to enable the gears to be changed with the right foot, as would be familiar to Western riders in this era, and a British-made Smiths Industries rev counter – in the early days Honda used many British-made smaller components, before later developing their own. Interestingly, the aluminium fairing has been cut away behind the front wheel to provide better airflow to the engine, as a way to overcome the overheating that was found to be a problem. The machine is still in running order and is still paraded by the museum at historic motorcycling events.

A newcomer to the Honda team in 1961 was Michihiko Aika, better known in later years as 'Aika San'. In the mid-1950s he had transferred from the production line at Honda to support the racing side of the operation, and this was his first year as a mechanic with the Grand Prix squad. Later he would go on to manage the team as Chief Mechanic. In order to increase the level of experience within the company as a whole, Honda would frequently rotate mechanics through the race team. However, to call these people mechanics would be in many cases be a misnomer, for numbers of them were university engineering students with Honda sponsorship.

It is no exaggeration to say that Honda's success in this event, followed of course by the emergence of Suzuki, Yamaha and Kawasaki, signalled the end of the British motorcycle industry, which had for a long time been too complacent in the face of growing foreign competition. Prophetically, one British newspaper ran a story in the wake of the 1961 Honda victories that stated:

> The Rising Sun of Japan blazed brightly over the TT races at the Isle of Man last week, as Japanese motorcycles won the first five places in both the 125cc and 250cc events. How did the Japanese manufacturers – whose machines were competing at the Isle of Man for only the third time – achieve their spectacular success? To find the answer, a British motorcycle firm stripped down one of the Japanese machines. What they discovered spells a grim warning to Britain's motorcycle exporters. This is what the British firm's works director said: 'When we stripped the machine, frankly, it was so good it frightened us. It was made like a watch and it wasn't a copy of anything. It was the product of original thinking and very good thinking.'[20]

In just three short years Honda had gone from complete unknowns to worldwide success, with Australian Tom Phillis going on to take the 1961 125cc World Championship, and Mike Hailwood taking the 250cc crown, Honda's first major Grand Prix titles. Taniguchi remembered:

> In 1961 after gaining the top five positions in the 125cc and 250cc the team, their family and friends were treated by the company to a slap-up meal. It was a special time. In just three years we'd shot to number one! At that time 125cc and 250cc were the most popular and important bikes. Today there are 1,000cc bikes etc, but back then

> 350cc and 500cc bikes were not as popular. All the different companies concentrated their energies on the 125cc and 250cc. That's why our domination in 1961 was so important to Honda and Japan.[21]

This, however, was only the start, as Honda would go on to dominate every class of top-flight solo motorcycle racing before the decade's end.

Chapter Three

1962–63

THE RISE OF REDMAN

It appeared that at least one record was going to be broken by Honda before the 1962 TT races had even got under way, for the Isle of Man Steam Packet Company vessel bringing competitors across from Liverpool to Douglas that year carried no fewer than twenty-four Honda works machines. Jim Redman and some of the Honda technicians aboard chatted to journalists also making the crossing, informing them that six more machines (125cc production racers) had been sent on ahead, while another ship, the *Manx Maid*, making her maiden voyage and due to dock later, was carrying Bob McIntyre, who was bringing his own 285cc machine down from Scotland. That made a grand total of thirty-one works machines on the Island, a figure that has almost certainly never been surpassed by any other factory team either before or since. The haul contained seven brand new four-cylinder machines of both 250cc and 285cc capacity, which were almost identical in appearance and only distinguishable by their serial numbers. These seven had been fitted with somewhat ungainly 36-litre (8-gallon) fuel tanks, intended for use in the six-lap Lightweight and Junior events. It was envisaged that the tanks would allow their riders to complete the race without stopping for fuel. However, both Redman and Phillis made no secret of the fact that they were against the idea, the former pointing out to reporters that carrying some 60lb of fuel on board on the first lap would be more of a handicap than a mid-race fuel stop. The new four-cylinder models were also fitted with improved front brakes.

Far from being disgruntled with Hailwood for beating their own factory riders at the TT the previous year, it seems that Honda wanted to see the relationship continue, and would probably have supplied him with another machine or machines for 1962. However, Mike at this time had his heart set on riding for MV Agusta, and so consequently Ecurie Sportive did not approach Honda again. Apparently this upset the leadership of the Japanese firm, which had an unwritten rule that if a rider walked away from them there was no going back. Bob McIntyre did continue with the Honda works team at the TT in 1962, but was beset by mechanical problems and was a retirement in both the Lightweight and Junior races. He was to be killed tragically later in 1962 in an accident at Oulton Park. The Lightweight TT on the Monday of Race Week that year was won by another satellite rider, Kent's Derek Minter (known as 'the Mint'), using a 250cc machine from the previous season, fitted with one of the locally made larger-capacity fuel tanks. This underlined the point that machines supplied to privateers were every bit as good as those used by the factory teams, even though Minter was not wholly familiar with the bike. Before the race he told reporters:

> Apparently people have told me, the boys who ride them, that they will go up to sixteen [thousand rpm] if you get into any difficulty, if anybody is in front of you and you want to catch 'em they will go up to sixteen, but … that's a lot of revs to me and I'm frightened of it![1]

The story goes that before the start, Minter had been told that Jim Redman was a certainty to win; believing that he

Right: Soichiro Honda as a young man, in the 1920s. (Author's Collection)

Below: A cartoon from the *Isle of Man Examiner*'s 1959 TT Special; the Japanese team were the butt of numerous jokes like this; JAP engines of course were made by the British firm of J.A. Prestwich. (Author's Collection)

Above: Honda team minibus outside the Nursery Hotel in Onchan, 1959. (Naomi Taniguchi via John Dalton)

Below: Team talk among the Honda riders at the Nursery Hotel, 1959. (Naomi Taniguchi via John Dalton)

Above: Taniguchi signing autographs for local children at the Nursery Hotel. (Naomi Tanaguchi via John Dalton)

Right: The statue of Kunihiko Akiyama at Gotokuji, west of Tokyo, looking towards the Isle of Man. (Author's Collection)

Akiyama's gravestone. The letters TT are visible among the Katakana script. (Author's Collection)

Tom Phillis, of Sydney - Honda's first professional rider. (Author's collection)

Bob Brown, the Australian who rode for Honda in 1960. (Courtesy of Manx National Heritage PG-12100-74)

Above: Bob McIntyre at Quarterbridge in the 1962 Lightweight TT, one of the best performances of his career. (Author's Collection)

Below: Derek Minter, whose brief Honda career resulted in a win the 1962 Lightweight TT. (Courtesy of Iris Burden)

A Honda advertisement from 1962 draws on the firm's success at the Isle of Man TT. (Courtesy of Honda Europe/Courtesy of Mortons Media)

Honda satellite rider Bruce Beale stops for fuel in the 1965 Junior TT race. The Rhodesian rider was a protege of Jim Redman. (Nigel McClatchey, courtesy of Lisa Noakes)

was a better rider than Redman ever would be, Minter set out to prove his point. McIntyre, at least initially, was not going to let him have it all his own way, however, and after a good performance in Practice Week was considered to be the favourite. Before the race the Scot commented:

> Well I should think that this year I should have as good a chance as I had last, there doesn't appear to be very much opposition to the Hondas this year, but I think it's an open race and there's about four or five of us all capable of winning.[2]

Another strong contender was Phillis, but he appeared resigned to the fact that he would be chasing 'Mac':

> Yes I think that's it and I think he will do the hundred miles an hour this year, I think he can do it, certainly, and we're hoping that all the Hondas will run well, and if they do I'm sure that he'll do it, so then my object must be to try and do the same thing.[3]

When the flag dropped at 1.30pm Hailwood and Minter led the field away. Phillis was behind them, and ten seconds further back, his machine already hinting at a misfire as he pulled away from Jim Redman and Japanese teammate Kitano in the next pairing. Phillis's Honda would run better later in the race, after he had pulled into the pits for a change of plugs and a switch to smaller jets, but the stop cost him five minutes and put him out of serious contention. There was some speculation that Honda had issued team orders and wanted the Japanese rider to take the win, but Redman had assured reporters before the race that this was not so, and it was a complete free for all. At Ballacraine Minter was leading on the road, followed by Hailwood and McIntyre. By Kirk Michael the Flying Scotsman had closed up to Minter. By Sulby, McIntyre was leading by thirty seconds. On corrected time the order was McIntyre, Redman, Minter and Phillis. By the Mountain Box McIntyre had passed Minter and was leading on the road; coming past the Grandstand he posted a lap of 99.06mph from a standing start, but by Barregarrow it was all over for Mac as engine trouble forced him to pull in; a broken contact breaker spring – a component costing pennies – had laid low one of the most technologically advanced motorcycles of the 1960s.

This promoted Redman to first place, though Minter was first on the road. By the fifth lap, Minter had snatched the lead, when Redman was slow to leave the pits after refuelling – his engine sounding suspiciously as if it had lost its edge and was misfiring. Minter continued to extend his lead over Redman and by Keppel Gate he had more than a minute in hand over the Rhodesian. At the start of the final lap Minter streaked past the Grandstand but Redman pulled in again for fuel. Reports filtered back from the Honda mechanics that his fuel tank cap was faulty and kept coming open, spraying him with petrol and necessitating the extra stop. Minter never put a foot wrong for the remainder of the race, and took a convincing victory. Apart from his forehead being plastered with flies, he reported a trouble-free ride, describing it to reporters as 'smashing'. He even thanked Redman for spurring him on when he momentarily passed him! Interestingly 'the Mint' himself was later rather dismissive of the win, writing afterwards:

> My main ambition now, having achieved a good many I started out with, is to win the Senior TT in the Isle of Man. I'd just love to do that … It was always an ambition of mine to win a TT but when I did it in the 250cc the prestige wasn't really there, as my success was on a

> Japanese machine. So now I'd really like to win the Senior on a British bicycle – on one of my Nortons.[4]

Minter himself admitted freely that he could be over-sensitive – he once walked away from a race meeting because the man on the gate hadn't realised who he was – and the fact that he didn't secure a permanent ride with Honda rankled more than he was perhaps prepared to admit. He added:

> [I can't help] being frank and outspoken. But I honestly believe that this is one reason why I've never really had the chance of a good works contract in recent times. It could be argued that my place ought to have been safe in the Honda team after winning the 1962 TT, but my face didn't seem to fit.[5]

For Honda however the 1962 Lightweight was another 1-2-3, with Redman and Phillis on the podium along with Minter, but the 100mph lap in this class still eluded them. A new Honda rider, Tommy Robb, was now about to make his mark at the TT. Robb had grown up in Belfast wishing to emulate local road racing hero Artie Bell, who had been a Norton rider between the wars. He was an apprentice fitter and turner with Short Brothers and Harland when he first became involved in trials riding. He soon switched to road racing, competing in the many events held in Northern Ireland on public roads, before moving on to English short circuits. Robb made his first TT appearance in 1958, and by 1959 he achieved impressive results at the Ulster Grand Prix. In the 125cc race on the Isle of Man that year, aboard a Ducati he had finished between the Hondas of Taniguchi and Tanaka. In 1960, however, he suffered a setback when he broke his neck in a crash in TT practice. Robb's career was subsequently restarted by a link up with Spanish firm Bultaco, which offered him a factory ride and led ultimately to a deal with Honda. He remembered:

> Based on my results in the preceding years, my name was put forward to Honda Japan, by the great ex-works Norton rider and TT winner of the '40s/50s, Artie Bell who was also the Honda Distributor in Northern Ireland at the time. I then received a letter from Mr Kawashima in Japan, at the time Honda Race Director and team manager, offering me machines in the 50cc and 125cc classes with the option to upgrade to the 250 and 350 classes at a later date if required. Needless to say I had to consider this offer for nearly two seconds before sending off my reply. At the time I was contracted to the Spanish Bultaco Company in Barcelona but Senor Bulto, the owner, released me immediately, as he said my World Championship chances were greater riding for Honda than staying with Bultaco. I was amazed at Senor Bulto's kindness and later in my career went back to them.
>
> I realised how good the Hondas were, due to the results they had achieved in 1960 and 1961. … [in 1962] I managed to finish runner-up to teammate Jim Redman in the 350 World Championship ahead of the greatest of them all, Mike Hailwood, on his MV. During my period with Honda I was very proud to have finished in the first six in the 50cc-125cc-250cc and 350cc World Championships.
>
> I certainly found my time with these wonderful people to be very constructive and rewarding. Honda were quite remarkable to work with and would discuss all aspects of the machine with us on a regular basis. They also carried

> out any alterations we would suggest in double-quick time, in fact Honda would do everything in their power to see that we had the best machines to win races.
>
> I can honestly say that all my Honda rides in the TT were memorable but finishing 2nd in the 1962 125cc and 3rd in the 50cc races were indeed enjoyable.[6]

If a second place was good for Robb, then the 125cc race on the Wednesday morning would produce even better results for Taveri – it was the achievement of his greatest ambition, because he had been trying for seven years to conquer the Ultra-Lightweight class. He had scored third places in 1957 and 1960, and second places in 1955, 1959 and 1961. In the process he had broken the class lap record three times, but nothing could match what he accomplished on this day, placing the first ever 125cc lap at over 90mph to bring a gaggle of Hondas home in first, second, third, fourth and fifth places. The only real opposition came from Mike Hailwood aboard a water-cooled EMC, but his challenge ended in the final lap with engine trouble. Behind Taveri it was an all-Honda battle between Redman, Robb, and Kunimitsu Takahashi mounted on works machines, and Tom Phillis and Derek Minter on the new production bikes. These were of the CR93 model, available for the first time that year (CR standing for Customer Racer). It had twin cylinders and had a five-speed gearbox. The type was developed from a Honda road bike, as evidence of which there was a blanked-off hole on the engine where a kick starter would ordinarily have been found. Honda claimed that these machines produced 16.5bhp but it was well known that they produced much more; 22bhp was not unknown. They were also tough and extremely reliable; consequently, they were very popular among privateers. Tom Phillis compared it with his usual ride and noted that:

> This one has a five-speed gearbox against the six, and it's missing a few horsepower at the top end, but they've spread the power more in this one, so that the five-speed box is quite useful on it, and you don't notice the drop in revs between the gears, and also it seems to give a good performance, although it doesn't accelerate quite as savagely as the racing 125, which is now becoming quite a fast machine …[7]

It might well have been an all Honda top six in this race were it not for the fact that Takahashi crashed at Union Mills on the first lap and was seriously injured. Arguably the most successful of the Japanese riders recruited by Honda during the 1960s, he had already won four Grands Prix at other circuits (in the process becoming the first Japanese rider to win a race at World Championship level) and Honda had hoped that he would become the first Japanese rider to win a TT. He had made his debut as a motorcycle racer in 1958 and joined Honda two years later. Takahashi never really recovered from his injuries that day, even though a Japanese professor of surgery was sent to Europe to treat his complicated pelvic fracture (Keiko Carran again proving herself invaluable in liaising between the professor and Manx medical staff). Although Takahashi was to remain in the Honda squad for another couple of years, he subsequently switched to four-wheeled racing. Taveri gave an account of this dramatic race in his memoir, *My Life on Two Wheels*:

> The next round of the season was the Tourist Trophy. This greatest and most difficult race should bring an

important preliminary decision in the battle for the World Championship for 125cc machines. That preliminary decision was to be in my favour, but it didn't really make me very happy because my Japanese teammate Takahashi had a serious accident at this meeting. Takahashi led in the World Championship rankings after his victories at Barcelona and Clermont. Jim Redman was also in a very good position with two second places. For me, the TT meant the last opportunity to find my form, because I didn't just want to show the Honda factory that the right man had got the contract with a Grand Prix victory, I wanted to be World Champion!

Honda had stationed almost two dozen mechanics on the Island. But this contingent was hardly enough to supervise the eleven factory riders: Redman, Phillis, McIntyre, Robb, Minter, Takahashi, Tanaka, Taniguchi, Shimasaki, Kitano and Taveri. The poor guys had to work almost day and night. The workshop was at times a battlefield, so many machine parts were lying around.

It is, of course, important to ride a race track as often as possible to get to know it well. With the TT this is not a little thing, because a lap measures 64 km. You need about twenty-five minutes to cover this distance. If you ride quickly, you can cover four laps on a practice day, but you have to use every minute. Like many other riders, I got up early, even in the dark of night, at the start of the practices. This was so as not to lose anything from the precious practice time, because I had every necessity to memorise the pitfalls of the course.

I achieved the best practice time, 1.5 seconds faster than Takahashi. In the race – it took place on a Wednesday – I had to start 20 seconds behind the Japanese rider. We passed Bray Hill, Quarter Bridge, Union Mills. Then

> suddenly I saw the marshals swing their flags excitedly. It was not easy for me to control my machine past a rider that lay on the ground. I realised that it was a Honda. The words, 'That can only be Takahashi', shot through my head. On the next lap I saw the smashed machine standing against a wall: it clearly carried Takahashi's number. One of my most dangerous opponents was eliminated. But I didn't have the victory in my pocket for a long time. It was still necessary to beat Redman, Phillis and the Suzukis.
>
> The TT is a murderous race. It places incomparably high demands on the rider and machine. My main concern now was to get over the whole distance of 192km without a problem. But I could rely on my Honda.
>
> I won the race by a pretty big margin over Robb, Phillis, Derek Minter and Redman, all on Hondas. Honda achieved a fivefold success, although their strongest man (on paper form at any rate) Takahashi had failed. I learned after the race that the Japanese rider was seriously injured in hospital.[8]

Things were all set now for the Junior race that same afternoon. It was one of the most open events for many years, indeed any one of five makes of machinery stood a chance of winning, and few were confident enough to speculate on who would actually claim victory. After their retirements in the previous race, Honda had been granted special permission to weigh their machines in late for the Junior, in order to give them more time to sort out technical glitches – misfiring to be precise. It was the first time that Honda had competed in this class, and the machines that the team had entered for it were originally 250cc, bored out to 285cc. However at 10.10pm on Tuesday night, instead of the three motorcycles of Redman,

Phillis and McIntyre, only the latter two appeared, Redman being a non-starter.

The 1962 Junior TT was destined to be memorable for all the wrong reasons, and the dark side of the Mountain Course showed its face when Honda team leader Tom Phillis was killed in a crash at Laurel Bank on the second lap. Phillis was liked by everyone – it was not just his laid-back attitude to life that won him friends; his abilities on a racing motorcycle won him admiration as well. Tragically he was not even supposed to have been competing in this race – it was his machine that had failed on the Tuesday night, not that which Redman was slated to ride. The greatest challenge in the Junior was set to come from the MVs of Mike Hailwood and Gary Hocking, and Phillis was itching to take them on. Some have since claimed that even though Phillis was the reigning 125cc World Champion at the time, he felt that his position at Honda was not secure, and that he had something to prove. Despite the fact he was riding in the 125cc and 250cc he asked Redman if he would stand aside and let him ride in this one as well. The Rhodesian rider agreed, and on race day he accompanied Phillis to the start line, before becoming a spectator at the bottom of Bray Hill. The two chatted casually for a few minutes, Redman reportedly telling him to take it easy and the race would be his. Phillis is said to have replied that you couldn't have it both ways. These would be his last words.

At the end of the first lap Hocking and Hailwood, followed closely by Phillis, came hurtling through. The Honda was bouncing around on the road as he battled to keep up with the leaders. Inevitably he took more risks as he tried to stay with them, and suddenly his name was missing from the Tannoy commentary. Redman knew instantly from the expression on the face of team manager Reg Armstrong that Tom was dead. New Zealander Hugh Anderson was also a member of the

'Continental Circus' as Grand Prix riders were known at this time, and was friendly with Phillis. Shockingly he was the first on the scene of the accident:

> Although he was the current 125 World Champion he (Tom) was being used as a support rider only by Honda. Being a very determined and serious competitor, Tom was obviously out to prove a point in the 350cc TT riding a virtually untested, new, poor-handling 285cc Honda in its first race. Hailwood (MV) caught Tom just 11km from the start, then Hocking caught and passed both of them on the Mountain. At the end of the first lap they screamed through the start as one. Just 2.8 seconds covered them. Obviously Tom was trying very hard to stay with the two brilliant MV riders. But they were on vastly superior machines. My race number was 16 so I started 1 minute 10 seconds after Tom. On the second lap I rode past an accident at Laurel Bank. The marshals had yet to arrive. It was Tom. He was still partially on the bike, his right leg draped over the seat and his head under the front wheel. A small puddle of oil had formed under the Honda's engine and a trickle of blood ran from under the front wheel. Tom was dead.[9]

In the commentary box, seasoned TT reporter Graham Walker reportedly wept openly at the news of Tom's accident. His wife Betty was in the Grandstand, waiting for him to return, with their young son, christened Braddan after his father's favourite part of the course. She never got over his death, though she admitted she would not have even tried to stop him racing as it was his life's passion. After he had been cremated and his ashes scattered near the start line on Glencrutchery Road, she returned to Australia with their children. Times were hard for her financially without her husband's income, but Honda stepped in to make sure that she could afford to bring up the children. Redman was so shattered by the loss of his friend that he was ready to give up racing and return home, but he was persuaded by other riders to come to terms with what had happened. He was subsequently promoted to team leader in place of Phillis.

In 1962 a new class was added to the TT schedule, the 50cc race, as part of a 50cc World Championship series. For some enthusiasts and purists, what became known as the 'Tiddler' race was an insult to a race meeting of the stature of Isle of Man TT, but it was particularly attractive to Japanese factories because unlike the situation in Europe and the United States, in many parts of Asia 50cc machines had a large, if not dominant, share of the mainstream motorcycle market. Nevertheless, many of the doubters were won over by the incredible speeds of which these tiny-capacity machines proved themselves capable. Ulsterman Tommy Robb was recruited by Honda for this and other classes. In the early part of the 1962 season, in the Spanish and French Grands Prix the Honda 50cc machine, though well up on power, was falling behind those of Suzuki and Kreidler. This was because the little machines simply did not have enough gears to make the best use of their power output. An intense long-distance telephone conversation followed between race team management and company headquarters. In response, the factory in Japan had produced a new eight-speed gearbox in a matter of weeks. By the time of the Isle of Man TT in May, a ten-speed gearbox was in development and in the middle of Practice Week, two freshly designed 50cc machines (designated model RC111) arrived on the Island, replete with the new transmission, one each for Robb and Taveri. This was just as well because Suzuki's Ernst Degner was the hot favourite to win this race. Robb, in an interview just before the race, described how these machines handled on the faster parts of the course:

> Well its rather deceptive because you don't get the same impression of speed that you do on a 500, obviously, and yet you're probably going within maybe forty to fifty mile an hour off the top speed of a 500, but when you got to stop, you realise that you've got very small brakes, and they're very lightweight to get stopped … But I should say that the feeling of speed is in the actual cranking over into the corners … you've got the tendency to lift it out rather than lean it up the camber …[10]

Derek Minter was also mounted on a Honda machine for this race. He remembered:

> It's marvellous, I've never ridden such an enjoyable bicycle in all my life. You can really have fun with it, you can rush through corners flat out with it and no worry at all … it's only tiring in one process, and that's your neck; I'm afraid so, your neck gets rather battered about from being on the tank for so long, in trying to look where you're going, it does give you a pain in the back of your neck … From Kate's [Cottage] to the Creg I'll be doin' a hundred miles an hour, and from Creg to Brandish I should think I'd be doin' a hundred miles an hour.[11]

Degner was first away, followed by Minter and Ichino. The East German rider streaked ahead of the competition, increasing his lead lap by lap. Taveri finished second – and Robb third – behind his Suzuki, thanks to the better spread of power provided by the ten-speed gear shift, but Degner had broken Honda's growing stranglehold on the smaller-capacity classes. Despite the tragic loss of such an important rider as Tom Phillis, 1962 was a hugely successful season for Honda, with three individual riders' World Championships to their name by the end of it, and three constructors' championships. The 125cc crown went to Taveri, with Redman taking the honours at the 250cc and 350cc levels.

In 1963 the Honda company stepped up its development of four-wheeled racing vehicles. Without limitless resources at its disposal, this inevitably meant that that there would be reduced funding and personnel for the motorcycle Grand Prix squad. Honda withdrew from the 50cc class, though remained committed to 125cc, 250cc and 350cc competition, albeit using a combination of the previous year's racing machines and some production bikes. At the same time, there was increasing pressure from other manufacturers, notably old rivals Suzuki, and up and coming concern Yamaha, who were just starting to hit their stride. Tommy Robb remembered:

> In 1963 Honda adopted a low-key approach to road racing and didn't produce the same 100 per cent works machinery they had the previous year. They lent us what became known as production racers, 125cc and 250cc twins, and later in the year they introduced the 305cc twin. In the world championship meetings we still had the 250cc 'fours', while Jim Redman rode the 350cc 'four' backed up by Luigi [Taveri] and me on the less-powerful 305s. I certainly didn't get as much satisfaction out of this year as I did in 1962, when it was full-blown works racing all the way.[12]

The first solo race of the week on the Isle of Man was the 250cc Lightweight event. Somewhat poorly supported in the previous two years, this time around there was a much stronger field, indicating a revival of interest in this class. Tommy Robb and Jim Redman were on four-cylinder 'works' machines for this race, with production 'twins' for Taveri and Kunimitsu Takahashi. Robb described the difference between the two:

> Surprisingly enough the new production machine is showing extremely good capabilities in its previous races, and I would say that, in acceleration there's very little to choose between the twin and the four, but in top speed, the four has probably got a little extra … maybe at the moment the four is handling a little better than the twin also, and should give it a little more advantage.[13]

Jim Redman remembered that while driving from his hotel on the Douglas Promenade up to the Grandstand on the day of the event, the heat created shimmering pools on the road surface. As he put on his tight-fitting leathers, the clammy heat intensified, giving him an idea of what conditions in the race would be like. With the works Suzukis and Alan Shepherd's MZ among the twenty-nine non-starters, the four Honda team riders headed the field away, with a clear road in front of them. First off the line was Tommy Robb, followed by Takahashi, Redman and then, further down the field, Taveri. The biggest challenge came from the Yamahas of Tony Godfrey and Fumio Ito. By the end of the first lap Ito was leading, the first time that a Japanese rider on a Japanese machine had held the lead in a TT race. Godfrey was not far behind, but Redman's Honda was gaining on them. Not long after the start things started happening, as rider after rider fell off in the tricky conditions. Others retired or were held up with mechanical issues; Taveri and Takahashi both quit mid race with engine problems. Tommy Robb pitted at the end of the first lap to change his plugs, costing him two minutes and twenty-five seconds, while Godfrey stopped at Kirk Michael to make adjustments. He too lost over two minutes before restarting – he then also came into the pits for a change of plugs, by which time he was completely out of the running. He nevertheless carried on with the race until he slid off at Milntown after his engine locked up, suffering severe head injuries. Ito continued to hold the lead as Redman picked his way around, avoiding the worst parts of the road as far as possible. However, he was having technical difficulties of his own. In the blistering heat his engine was getting hotter and hotter, burning his legs even through his leathers. The machine also appeared to be slowing on each lap. At the halfway pit stop the mechanics offered to try to identify the problem but Redman refused; after Ito suffered difficulties in his pit stop, he was now in the lead and wanted to be away as quickly as possible in order to try to hang on to it. After a swig of lemonade the Rhodesian rider roared away, his determination to win never stronger.

With teammates Taveri and Takahashi already out of contention, this left just Redman and Tommy Robb to carry the Honda colours, the latter holding fourth place until a second pit stop for plugs, this time costing him five minutes. For the final two laps Redman, by now leading by fifty seconds, rode as hard as he dared, the overheating engine causing agonising pain in his legs, until the fluttering flags of the Grandstand came into view for the last time. Robb caused gasps of amazement from the crowd as he came into the pits yet again at the end of the fifth lap, swerving as he applied the brakes too heavily and overshooting his mark. Tank replenished, Robb shot off to take fifth place. Despite his engine slowing, and his lead diminishing, the cheers and waving programmes told Redman all that he needed to know as he approached the chequered flag. He remembered afterwards:

> I realised one of my biggest ambitions at precisely 3.54pm on Monday, 10 June 1963. For on that searing hot afternoon in the Isle of Man I won my first ever TT … I had been racing there since 1958 and had never really shone on the circuit. It had become an obsession with me to win there. But I had to overcome my intense dislike of the course. And that took some doing. The race … was the 250cc. It was recorded in the newspapers as the 'Slip-'n-Slide TT'. The scorching sunshine, great for holidaymakers but hell for riders, had turned a lot of the circuit into a stream of bubbling, molten tar. It was dangerously slippy most of the way round.[14]

Amid the crowds of reporters and cameramen, his wife was waiting to hug him, as pleased and relieved as he was. His nightmare ride had turned into a dream come true. He told reporters afterwards:

> I soon realised the bike was not going so well as in practice, but it was chiming on all four. There was a lot of tar about, especially on all the bridges after Sunday's traffic and the Sidecar race so I took the first lap steadily. Then I got a signal that Ito was in front so I rushed on a bit quicker. There was a big puddle of tar in the road at the Les Graham Memorial. It seemed to get bigger and on lap four I had quite a slide. After that I rode round it. There was a flock of seagulls all over the road at Keppel Gate. About forty of them were just rising off the road as I arrived, so I ducked back under the screen in case I hit one! The bike was slowing towards the end and I knew

> Ito was closing up on me, but there was nothing I could do about it.[15]

Ito finished in second place, and third was taken by Bill Smith of Chester, on a privately entered production Honda, after a terrific performance during which he slid off at Governor's Bridge but gamely remounted and carried on, still holding his position. Speaking to Murray Walker in the winner's enclosure, Redman added:

> I had good signals, I knew [Ito] was close but the bike was slowing all the time and I couldn't go any quicker … I don't know [why], the engine just lost a few revs … but … I don't know what the trouble is.[16]

Redman's hesitancy under questioning suggested that he did know what the trouble was, but that being fully aware of the Honda Motor Company's obsession with secrecy, and a good factory rider, he did not want to give anything away publicly that might help a competitor. Honda had won, but only just. This was the slowest 250cc TT since 1960, and the writing was on the wall – if Honda could not pull more horsepower out of the bag then the following year Yamaha's name might well be inscribed on the trophy. But for Redman, that evening back at the team hotel it was all about celebrating his success. The mechanics and riders swapped stories and relived the race over and over again, but he could scarcely accept the fact that his name was to be inscribed onto one of the famous Mercury TT trophies – the greatest and most beautiful examples of such things in the sporting world.

After the heat of Monday, Wednesday of Race Week could not have dawned with a greater contrast. It was cold, wet and foggy. The first race in the morning was the 125cc event, and here the real favourites were a rejuvenated Suzuki team. Honda team captain Redman was unenthusiastic about the prospects for success in the coming race, stating:

> Well I thought that on this course, the Suzukis would probably not be reliable enough, and we would come through on our well-known reliability, but it just hasn't worked out. In practice the Suzukis have been going round doing three laps at a time, so it leaves us to beat them just in speed and I think that it's going to be very difficult.[17]

After a two-hour delay, the race finally got under way, and Hugh Anderson's Suzuki led at the end of the first lap, with Redman, Taveri and Robb chasing him, but it was a Suzuki 1-2-3 on the leader board. Mist on the Mountain was a problem in the beginning but as the race went on, visibility improved, allowing Hugh Anderson to go faster. His times were on average 5mph better than the fastest Honda. With a 1-2-3 on the podium and the team prize in the bag, Suzuki had well and truly trounced Honda in this race, proving beyond doubt the growing superiority of the two-stroke engine. Although Redman only managed sixth place, it at least gave him the advantage in the forthcoming 350cc Junior of knowing exactly how bad the conditions were around the course. As the 125cc race was ending the 350cc machines were already being warmed up. Redman's wife unstitched his black 125cc race patch from his leathers to reveal the blue 350cc number beneath, as he tried to warm himself with a cup of coffee before going out again to compete. This time his main opposition would be Mike Hailwood, mounted on an MV, who was setting off with him as the first pairing on the starting grid. Knowing how fast

Mike was on the Isle of Man, he decided that his best tactic would be to just stay with him for most of the race, and to try to pass him in the latter stages. Unlike the previous year when the firm had only been able to field bored-out stopgap machines, this time Redman was provided with a very businesslike RC172, which had already won the West German Grand Prix. He was enthusiastic about the new machine:

> Well of course I think it's a terrific motorbike, it proved it at Hockenheim, when I just sat on it and away it went and won the race at a terrific speed. It's quite a difficult bike to ride around here because it's very small and light, and goes very fast, so it's quite hard to hold down, I think the MV although it's slower would be easier to ride, it keeps straighter and handles better … I don't like to underrate any of [the opposition] but I do think that Mike is the chief opposition, and I think I'm fairly fortunate in starting with him. I think it's to my advantage more than it is his, to start together, one and two on the road, and I think it's going to be fairly hectic! … I don't like to plan before, but I think in the first lap I'll do my best to stay behind Mike, and then when I've seen how he does it perhaps I'll be able to get past him somewhere … I know at Hockenheim [the Gileras] didn't show very well, but then I do know that they weren't going at their best, and because they haven't gone awfully quick in practice, I don't think that that is as fast as they can go, I think that everybody in the 350 class has been foxing, and nobody has shown their real form.[18]

Redman was not the only rider to carry the Honda flag in this race; Tommy Robb would also participate on a 305cc machine, which in spite of its lower cylinder capacity had still managed to post the second fastest time in practice. He was certainly rated as in with a chance of winning the race. Robb was also positive about his chances aboard the machine:

> Well I think its main advantage is the fact that this is basically a machine with 350 and over 350cc power in a very lightweight frame, because it's a similar type frame to that used on the Production twin-cylinder 250cc models, and I think its power to weight ratio is so good that it scores here. [With] the first frame [we used] we were having a tendency to in effect whip itself in the frame on a particularly fast, bumpy corner; the new frames that have arrived for the Island are much more rigid with twin down tubes instead of the singular wishbone type that was on the original frame, and it has certainly cured this whipping to an extreme extent.[19]

One and half hours late, and with the Mountain still swirled in mist, the competitors in the Junior TT prepared to get under way. Even though the weather had cleared a little, the start line was still a sea of gloomy faces. This was the unique challenge of the Isle of Man, the unpredictable nature of the weather on the Island making it a course like no other. Redman was first away on the wet road, riding as hard as he dared. He expected to be challenged by Hailwood, or the Gilera-mounted duo of Read and Hartle of Scuderia Duke, the team put together by former World Champion Geoff Duke, but by Ramsey he was surprised to find himself ten seconds in the lead. Over the Mountain the mist was as thick as a bag, and in dropping back Hailwood caught and passed him at the start of the drop to Creg-ny-Baa. The two diced for the remainder of the lap. On the next circuit, the mist had cleared on the Mountain and

Redman was able to open up a lead of over twenty seconds on Hailwood. At the midway point the pair pitted at the same time. Redman's refuelling crew were marginally quicker and he left the pits first by just a few seconds. Hailwood was full of fight and roared away, mischievously sticking his tongue out at the Honda mechanics as he did so, but his engine gave up shortly afterwards, leaving him to coast back to the Grandstand. Redman was now on his own in the lead. All he had to do was stay on in order to win, but in the worsening conditions that was no mean task. Half expecting the race to be stopped, indeed hoping the race would be stopped (even though he was in the lead), grimly he pressed on, his leathers now soaked. His goggles steamed up and so he removed them, in spite of the stinging rain lashing his eyes. His worst moment came at Glen Helen on the last lap where the road was awash with a torrent of rainwater flooding across it. Redman got into a slide from which he was lucky to recover. It was his worst racing moment in a long time and he admitted that it shook him. He won by some six minutes, such was the attrition further down the field, but cold and cramped he was in no mood to celebrate. His fingers had almost become clamped to the handlebars with cold, his back was locked in a riding position and he could not feel his legs. He had to be helped off the bike. Speaking to Murray Walker after the race, he said:

> [It was] terrible … you couldn't see for rain and mist and fog and Lord knows what and I thought every lap that they were going to stop it, after the end of the fourth, and I was quite surprised they let us go through to the finish. [Mike Hailwood] was right up alongside me a few times, maybe he goes quicker over the Mountain, I know he was riding like a demon![20]

It was on the 305 machine in the Junior TT that Robb had another accident. The bike had developed an oil leak just before the start, but when it stopped the team manager allowed him to set off. He was under instructions to take things easy in case the leak should restart, and so he proceeded at a steady pace, with a number of riders passing him, in case the oil sprayed on to the rear tyre. By the time he reached Ramsey, he had a look behind, saw that the tyre was clean, and decided to speed up. Going at full race speed he made it as far as the Les Graham Memorial at the Veranda. Unfortunately in the heat of the previous day the tar had melted on the road at this point, and traffic passing over it had created a shiny patch, which was treacherous in the wet conditions. As Robb angled the bike over at this point it slid out from under him, and he was sent hurtling down the road.

The thin race suits of those days were designed more for providing slipstream than protection from gravel rash, and the chippings of the road surface tore the leathers away completely down one side of his body. Bloodied and bruised, his injuries also included a broken right finger. Over the Tannoy at the Grandstand came the less than accurate announcement: 'Number seven Tommy Robb has retired at the Graham Memorial, rider OK.' As he lay injured in the Les Graham shelter, Phil Read, who had broken down nearby, came to his assistance. Robb continues:

> They brought us back in the police ambulance, but as I was racing at Mallory on the Sunday I asked a policeman if he would let me pick up my van and I would meet him at the hospital. He agreed, and I said 'I'll see you there.' But I rushed back to my hotel, changed and headed off for the mainland with my finger lashed up in a most unprofessional manner. My finger's still out of shape![21]

Jim Redman, however, was in a better frame of mind than he had been after the Junior TT, as the ship left Douglas harbour carrying him away at the end of the week. With him were two beautiful full-sized Mercury trophies, his to keep for the year, and a wallet full of prize money. Things, however, were about to get more difficult for him, and his teammates. As part of their economy drive, halfway through the season Honda withdrew their mechanics from the race squad in order to save money. Luigi Taveri wrote ruefully:

> After the Tourist Trophy, the pitiful remains of the Honda team had already returned to Japan. For us, racing became even tougher, because now we were all alone. This explains why it was that I did not achieve very much in 1963.[22]

The riders were now effectively privateers and made their own arrangements for mechanics. Redman brought in fellow Rhodesian Nobby Clark, who had trained as a railway engineer before coming to Europe in 1960 to spanner for countryman Gary Hocking, while working as a car park attendant at Olympia exhibition centre in London to fund himself through the winter. Clark would remain with Honda through 1964, and recalled:

> What I remember most about the TT is the amount of work involved. It was no secret that we worked all night to get ready for morning practice. We'd be in two shifts: one would catch a couple of hours sleep whilst the other worked on. We'd do complete engine overhauls, change tyres every two practices (in the Sixties, tyres were expected to last a lot longer than in modern racing) and service the brakes, which were worked hard on

> the Mountain Course. It was easier for me than for the Japanese, because they had language problems and got fed up being away from home. But we all got a hell of a lot of satisfaction from winning a TT race.[23]

Although Tommy Robb was at first informed at the end of the season that he would be racing again for Honda in 1964, he was not given a full year's contract, and in fact this would be his last TT before switching to Yamaha. In many ways 1963 was an extraordinary year for Honda, for in spite of fielding one of the weakest teams of their 1960s campaign, with minimal investment, few new machines and indeed motorcycles that had been heavily campaigned the previous year, they still managed to secure two rider's World Championships, with Redman taking both the 250cc and 350cc titles, as well as a second place in the 125cc class. It was an amazing testament both to the superiority of the original designs, and to the longevity and resilience of the engines. Yet if Honda were to retain their dominance in top-flight motorcycle racing, they knew that they would need to bring something special to the table for 1964, because their rivals were advancing now at frightening speed. At the last race of the 1963 season, the Japanese Grand Prix, the Honda company revealed newly developed machines, in particular the 50cc RC113, which now featured four valves per cylinder, that would take the challenge for world dominance into the coming year.

Chapter Four

1964–65
TWO-STROKE CHALLENGERS

In 1964 Honda would face more of a challenge to its dominance that perhaps at any time since the firm stepped onto the world stage in motorcycle racing, as other Japanese firms raised their game in a bid to show that they too could claim a share of the glory. Also, the media focus in this year was beginning to shift away from the 500cc class, which had always been seen as the blue riband category, towards the smaller machines, particularly the 250s. Since the start of the decade, and certainly since he signed for MV Agusta, the 500cc class had been so heavily dominated by Mike Hailwood that in the eyes of many it had started to become a procession. Mike's MV was simply so powerful that he was really only racing the clock on many occasions. The newspapers and racing public had realised, however, that in the smaller classes there was now a real scrap going on, and things were much closer. Scuderia Duke had faded by this point in time, and Phil Read had been snapped up by Yamaha to ride their incredibly fast lightweight machines. Suzuki with their 250 square fours were also a constant threat, and MZ had now been granted permission by the East German government to race beyond the Iron Curtain, putting them in contention at many more circuits. However, while the other Japanese factories put their faith in two-stroke technology, Honda Motor Company remained utterly wedded to four-stroke machinery. Soichiro Honda could have taken the easier route to remaining competitive, and developed his own two-stroke engine, but he loathed these dirty, smoky, whining motors and had vowed never to stoop to making one. As he saw it, success was important, but so was integrity; the four stroke was the aesthetically more pleasing option and this was what the firm persevered with.

The problem for Honda was that the rules of racing took no account of this. In the 250 class, an engine's total cylinder capacity could not exceed 250cc, regardless of how many cylinders the engine had. So in order to compete with the much lighter two strokes, Honda were forced to add more cylinders and more gears to their engines. However, there were other advantages to this approach. In a five- or six-cylinder engine, the individual capacity of each pot was very small, so there was less compression and the engine was easier to turn over. In an era when riders push started their machines away from the line, this was an important consideration. Another problem for Honda stemmed from the fact that their semi-withdrawal from motorcycle racing in 1963 had created a certain amount of confusion over how committed they actually were to success in this sport. One of their star riders, Luigi Taveri, remembered:

> I had already had some negotiations with Kreidler, the German factory that participated exclusively in racing in the 50cc class. With the 50cc Hondas there was really nothing to gain, while Anscheidt on a Kreidler had won two Grands Prix in 1963. But I never signed a contract because I had always waited for Honda to provide me with better material. Now Kreidler approached me again and offered me an interesting deal for 1964. They had become wiser and didn't give me weeks to think … Since it looked

as if the Japanese factory would finally withdraw from racing, it would have been my intention to be signed by Kreidler. I got in touch with the Honda branch in Hamburg. They inquired in Japan, but could not tell me anything. Now it seemed clear; the best thing for me was probably an engagement at the Stuttgart plant [and] I signed the contract … It was easy to feel guilty: I felt as if I had betrayed Honda, the brand which had brought my success. Two weeks before the World Championship round, the Honda factory management ordered me to Japan. At the head of a delegation of several high-ranking employees, Mr Segiguchi received me at the airport. We called this kind older man 'Papasan'. We actually considered him the 'father' of the Honda team. As soon as they welcomed us, the Japanese began to talk about their great new machines.

East Asians – I knew this after two years of experience – are very reserved. These motorcycles had to be really extraordinary if they spoke of them in such tones. A 50cc engine with two cylinders and a 125cc with four, both with four valves per cylinder and a speed of 18,000 rpm – something that had never existed before. I couldn't wait to look at the machines. The next day we flew to Suzuka. There I was proudly presented with the 'wonders of Japanese technology'. And they were really miracles! The Japanese are wronged by those who say that they only know how to copy European or American products. These 'copies' – just one of many examples – far surpassed any 'original'. My heart beat faster when I heard the two engines running. The Japanese looked at me and expected praise for their constructions.

Of course, I thought the two new designs were wonderful, but the Honda people did not know that I had already

> missed the chance to ride this unique motorcycle next year, and I was gripped by an indescribably bad feeling … It was not an easy situation until I had made this clear to the Japanese! They were very disappointed. 'Now we've developed a machine like this and we can't use it in races because we don't have a rider who knows how to handle it.' I wanted to clarify why I had signed with Kreidler, but it was not possible for me to make the deeply disappointed Japanese understand my considerations that had led to this decision … At least I got a contract for the 125cc class. At the same time, Redman signed his contract. The Rhodesian was also tasked with looking for a young rider (as a 'Taveri replacement') capable of riding the 50cc Honda to victory.[1]

So it was that for the 1964 TT the little-known Irish rider Ralph Bryans, a 50cc specialist, also joined the Honda squad. Fellow Ulsterman Tommy Robb had already been released from his contract by this point and was now riding against Honda and his old teammates under the Yamaha banner. Original Honda team member Naomi Taniguchi also returned briefly to the squad, to compete in the 50cc class only. Jim Redman recounted later that in 1964:

> We had been worried by the sudden, dramatic upsurge of our Japanese rivals, Suzuki and Yamaha. They had suddenly come on like a bomb and had been handing out one or two beatings to me and the rest of the Honda team. We were determined to hit back TT week.[2]

Redman described how the greatest gamble of the week was not taking place at the Palace Casino on Douglas seafront, where dinner-jacketed men and sequinned women played roulette or blackjack in the evenings, but underneath it. For here was the garage that Honda had rented to prepare their race machines. To get into the game they had entered thousands of pounds worth of racing machinery, but at stake if the gamble came off were millions of pounds in sales of road-going motorcycles on the high street. He continued:

> I feel I must pay tribute to the Honda mechanics who worked ceaselessly to put the machines in unbeatable, tip-top condition. Here was the real teamwork – behind the scenes. The pity is that few people realise the work and the hours these boys put in. The midnight oil they burned was the real stuff. They were virtually prisoners in the garage and workshop we had hired for the TT. But they didn't mind or complain about the work. They knew, as well as any of the riders, that we were counter-attacking the Yamaha and Suzuki strongholds.[3]

The mechanics virtually lived in that garage, only coming up occasionally for a few hours' sleep. They even ate and drank in the garage with an improvised table laid out, to which smart waiters with bow ties delivered meals from the hotel kitchens above. A newspaper reporter coined the phrase 'Cellar Full of Secrets' to describe the place, and he was right. Security in the garage was tight – no one was allowed down the steps from the dining room who might be able to photograph the stripped-down engines and thus give an opposing team an advantage. Hotel doormen were asked to be especially vigilant in this regard. If any unauthorised person did manage to make it down from the hotel above, dustsheets or coats would quickly be thrown over the motorcycles within to shield them from prying eyes.

As an indicator of the importance that Honda attached to the 1964 Isle of Man TT, and how seriously they took the challenge from the opposition, on the Sunday morning of Practice Week a specially chartered plane that had travelled from Japan landed at Ronaldsway Airport on the Island, carrying six brand new racing machines and a number of engines, including three brand new twin-cylinder 50cc units. Two of the machines were improved 350cc motorcycles, two were brand new 250cc models, one with a modified front brake, a 125 and a 50cc. The precious cargo was superintended by Aika-San, Honda's chief race mechanic. By Monday of Practice Week, Jim Redman was already out practising on one of the 350s, and despite pulling in at Creg-ny-Baa with clutch trouble, reported that he was very pleased with its improved performance.

In the 1964 250cc World Championship Redman was embroiled in a battle for points with his Yamaha-mounted rivals, and he came to the TT as very much the underdog, with Phil Read hotly tipped to win this event. Nevertheless, he was not worried, and undertook the job in hand. By this time he had developed a technique for starting his machines that few of his rivals had noticed; in those days it was considered normal for riders to mount from the left, a hangover from horse-riding days. However, Redman pushed and jumped on from the right as this required one fewer step before he swung his leg over. He had also learned to apply the front brake and press forward on the front forks just before the flag dropped, as when released this had the effect of making the machine jump forward.

The first solo race of the week was the 250cc Lightweight TT race on the Monday afternoon. It saw a record entry of ninety-five riders on twenty-one different makes of machine. Ten factory teams were represented, and there were six previous TT winners on the starting grid. Honda had three competitors in the race, these being Redman, Luigi Taveri and Isamu Kaseya. The new Honda machines were described by Redman:

> Our new fours are lower, lighter, narrower, faster, and since I got beaten at the Spanish and the French [Grands Prix] they flew over two new bikes for the TT which are exactly the same as the ones I used at the Spanish and French, but I think they've put a lot more work into them, in the finer tuning of them, and one in particular is going well, and that's the one I've picked to ride … They are exactly the same to look at, the engines are exactly the same, the frames, everything is the same, but I think possibly they've just scratched around inside and found one or two mile an hour coming up here and there … [the Yamaha] is very fast, accelerates quicker than the Honda, and it will be a tough nut to crack. I don't know about reliability, I know that they've had a lot of trouble in practice because I've seen them on the side of the road, so possibly the Honda may score on reliability, but on speed if it comes to an out and out race and we all go the distance I think that the Yamahas are going to be the ones we're going to be up against.[4]

From this this machine, the 2RC164, Honda had squeezed every additional ounce of power that they could find. They had lightened everything that they could, and at 14,000 rpm it produced 50bhp, but this was the maximum that a four-cylinder engine of this capacity could achieve. Even so, it was still an impressive testament to Honda's development over five years; having started out as the RC160, this last incarnation of the four-cylinder engine developed something like 32 per cent more power than the original design.

Once the race got under way the lead swapped between Redman and Read in a thrilling dice. Read suffered a setback on the second lap when he had to pull in to have his spark plugs changed, setting him back more than a minute, but by the fourth lap, riding out of his skin he had clawed it back and roared into the lead. It was not to be Read's day, however, and a few minutes later on Bray Hill and at full pelt his engine seized. Luckily he was aware of it beginning to happen and put the clutch in, thus avoiding potentially being thrown off and allowing the machine to coast to a halt at Quarter Bridge. After trying briefly to restart the motor, Read walked away in disgust.

After 200 gruelling miles of racing, Redman was now back in the lead and only 14 miles remained to run. As he approached Ramsey Hairpin he lined his machine up for the sharp left-hander and began to bank, the rear of the machine slewed away in an alarming fashion and it took all of Redman's lightning reactions and skill to steer into the skid and bring it back upright. He discovered later that an oil seal had failed and had sprayed the left side of the rear tyre with lubricant, so that it could not grip when banked over. The problem became steadily worse and the leaking oil covered his boot, meaning that his foot kept slipping off the brake. In spite of all this, he not only won but set a new race record in the process. Afterwards he told Murray Walker:

> The bike went very well all through the race except for a slight oil leak that started on the second lap. I did put a lot of care into all the left-hand corners after that and probably took the edge off quite a bit. I could see [the oil] on my boots and on the exhaust pipe, and the tyre I thought must have some on it.[5]

In an interview published in *Octane* magazine (October 2006 issue) Jim recalled:

> Most of the time I never really knew the exact details of the bikes I rode, because we would mix frames, engines and other parts from different machines until we had a combination that worked – but in 1964 things were a little different. The 250cc RC164 was really only intended as a temporary measure, a stand-in until the six-cylinder bike was ready, but I ended up using it for most of the season.[6]

'RC164-103' was ridden by Jim Redman for almost the entire 1964 campaign before he switched to the new six-cylinder version for the final two races. Jim finished second to Phil Read (Yamaha) that year in one of the most hotly contested championships in Grand Prix history. Riding 'RC164-103', he finished first in the Isle of Man TT and in the Dutch TT at Assen, and at the season's end 'RC164-103' was given to Jim by Mr Takahashi of Honda. Jim transported the machine to South Africa, where it remained in its shipping crate until 1998, when he was persuaded to bring it to Europe to display and run it at various revival events. When it was auctioned by Redman in 2006, it was accompanied by a letter from M. Maekawa, Manager of the Racing Department at Honda in Tokyo, which read in part:

> Dear Sir, I confirm that Mr Sekiguchi, Poppa San, received permission from Tokyo Head Office … that Mr Sekiguchi could give the machine, RC 164 103 to you to come back to your home. Please accept this machine as a present with our grateful thanks for your effort to try to win the 1964 World Championship on your Honda.[7]

One of only three complete four-cylinder machines of this particular type made by Honda, this example still has matching frame and engine numbers: 'RC164-103'. It is believed to be the only original motorcycle of its kind still in existence.

Redman was to be less lucky in the 125cc race, which was run later that week on Wednesday morning. This time the biggest threat came from the Suzuki machines of Hugh Anderson and Frank Perris, but the Honda plan was for Taveri and Redman to go all out from the start, in a bid to force the Suzukis out with blown engines if they tried to keep pace. In the practice sessions Taveri had posted an almost unbelievable 94.6mph. He was confident that his machine was up to the job in hand, telling Murray Walker:

> The four-cylinder 125 Honda I think is a very nice bike, and I like the bike very much. Also the new bike is much faster than last year's model … When the weather is good, I think in the race all will go faster than Practice, and I hope also I will go a little faster.[8]

It was not lost on the opposition that Taveri seemed to have the fastest machine in the Honda camp, with Suzuki rider Hugh Anderson admitting that the four-stroke Honda had a little more power coming out of corners, but was hopeful that his own team could close the gap if it could get the carburetor settings just right.

In the race itself Redman was the first Honda rider away, with Bryans next. As the flag dropped and Redman left the line, the Honda was misbehaving, firing on only three cylinders, and it was not until 2 miles out that the fourth pot kicked into life. He remembered later:

> At the start, I think I must have flooded the carburetors just a little too much – we're still not quite used to the

> new fours, and up to now I've had a mechanic on the grid to help. But on Wednesday I had to do it myself, and I probably over did it. Anyway. At first it would only run on three cylinders, and when I looked back at Quarter Bridge Ralph Bryans and Frank Perris were right behind me. I thought I'd had it, but then the bike picked up – possibly the heat from the other cylinders had cleared the flooded one – and away we went.[9]

Hugh Anderson's surprise retirement only 6 miles from the start removed a major threat to the Honda teamsters. Taveri was fourth on the roads at this point, but on corrected time would be in third at the end of lap one. By the 7-mile marker, at Ballacraine, Ralph Bryans and Frank Perris, who had started ten seconds behind, had almost caught Redman on the road. He put the hammer down to really give them a race, and by Ramsey when he looked behind he was alone. However:

> At the Hairpin, the Honda signalling station put out a board with a 'minus 5' on it – so I knew I was five seconds behind Ralph and Frank, but I had gained about four seconds on them since Ballacraine. So I had another go over the Mountain. This year, our 125s are so fast that my size and weight aren't such a disadvantage. In fact, on some parts of the course where you really have to fight the bike, they're an asset.
>
> At Governor's Bridge I got another signal telling me I was only two seconds behind Perris at Keppel Gate. On the second lap I screwed it on a bit more and at Ramsey they told me I was one second ahead of Frank. Towards the end of the lap the twist-grip began to work loose on the handlebar. This meant that I had to try to steady it with my index finger when I opened up. And when I shut

> off, the block carrying the twin throttle cables turned on the 'bar and jammed under the front brake lever.[10]

Redman was riding so hard that the pace that had forced Anderson to retire also led Perris to drop out with mechanical issues as planned. This left the third Honda man, Ralph Bryans, to ride on alone, after dicing with Perris most of the way. Bryans in fact had been lucky to stay on after he braked in an unexpected wet patch at Creg-ny-Baa, and the back of the machine had almost come round to meet the front. Redman, meanwhile, had also taken the lead from Taveri, who it was originally envisaged would win, before the handlebar problem began to intercede:

> This was costing me time so when I passed the pits at the end of two laps I was relieved to get the signal 'plus 8 Luigi: Frank out.' The loose twist grip wasn't really bad and I pressed on. But I knew that Luigi would be catching me, for I knew that I wasn't able to go quite as fast as I had done on the second lap.[11]

Taveri, it should be remembered, was in the stronger position to win the 125cc world championship that year, but when it came to the TT there were no team orders from Honda; it was the fastest man on the day who took the win. Luigi was well aware that in racing often the first and most important person you have to beat is your own teammate:

> [At this point] the lead in the 125cc World Championship belonged to me. Next, the Tourist Trophy should bring an important preliminary decision in the fight for the highest title in motorcycle sport. In Practice the best times were always achieved by Redman and myself. One needed

> to be no expert to forecast from it a forthcoming duel between us.[12]

However, in contrast with Redman's views, Taveri believed that his lighter build made a lot of difference. In fact, he thought that it possibly counted for 5mph in speed between the two Honda riders, and he caught Redman on the final lap. There was more to it than just a simple matter of weight, as the Swiss ace tells us:

> It was of course also clear to me that it would be a hard battle between the Rhodesian and myself. Fortunately, my brother Franz, who had come to Douglas with me, had a plan beforehand, of how I would be better able to find out about the course of the race than my opponents. During the race, Franz was in a pub called Ginger Hall. There with a stopwatch he recorded the times of Redman and me and passed them by phone through to the Honda team, which was 8km away at Ramsey Hairpin. Whilst Redman was shown the times from the last completed circuit, I had already got the times that Franz had recorded with his stopwatch half a lap later.
>
> The route was damp and I initially drove a little too carefully. When I passed the 'Grand Stand' for the last time, the pit crew showed me a signal: '-13 Redman'. 13 seconds behind! How should I catch up in the final lap? I would have loved to win the TT, for prestige reasons, but also to consolidate my top position in the World Championship classification. I wanted to get the last drops of performance out of the machine. I knew exactly what not to do: if you drive too fast for the conditions, something suddenly will go wrong. You commit small, stupid mistakes that cost one or two tenths of a second

each time. And once this series of events has started, you can't break out of it so quickly.

But this time it worked. Nothing went wrong, without the smallest mistake I got through to Ginger Hall and then to Ramsey Hairpin. I looked forward to the scoreboard: '-7 Redman.' So I had picked up six seconds in 16 miles. That was not enough. I continued to press the pace. If I would have had time for it – I would have been amazed at myself.

Of course, I was only interested in the goal: who won? Jim Redman and I stood in the finishers area. Both of the same mind, we waited for the announcement of the loud speaker. 'Will I become the first rider to win three races in a TT?" So the Rhodesian seemed to be thinking, having already won the 250cc race and with a good chance in the afternoon's 350cc class. The British radio reporter Walker came up to both of us and wanted to interview me. It was not a bad sign if he was interested in me first. Before he could even say one word, I asked him the question of who was the winner. 'You Luigi, by three seconds.' I could have thrown my arms around his neck. Redman was amazed and disappointed. He granted me the victory. But he had expected his triple triumph and almost lost his composure for a moment. Then Jim and I were looking for which records we might have broken in this TT. In the second circuit, he had set up a new lap record, which I immediately undercut with my self-surprising final lap. With an average of 148.280km/h, I also improved the class record for the race overall. Redman also remained under the previous maximum performance of Anderson.[13]

The race ended in a Honda 1-2-3 with Bryans in third place, and all three Hondas had broken the lap record. After commentator Murray Walker had revealed to Taveri in the winner's enclosure that he had won, he asked him for a few words for BBC listeners:

> The race is good, the bike is perfect, but for me it is very hard because Jim goes too fast for me![14]

Redman's disappointment at not grabbing his second win in Race Week was tempered by the knowledge that his teammate had gained valuable points in the World Championship campaign and he added:

> I had a good ride also, but I'm afraid the old man here went too quick for me! I had a signal in the first lap that Anderson was out, and on the second lap Perris [had gone]. I didn't know where Schneider was, but I got a signal at Ramsey, 'Honda 1-2-3' and I thought, 'Well, that should be alright.'[15]

Aside from the twist grip problem, Redman considered that the Honda had gone like a watch for the whole distance. Directly after the race, ACU officials wanted to strip down all three of the podium machines for scrutineering purposes. Redman, mindful that the Honda mechanics had been working twenty-three hours a day for the past week, pointed out that the machines were identical, and asked if only one could be taken apart to allow some of the Japanese technicians some rest. He felt that TT officials were sometimes too closely attached to the rule book, but on this occasion the Clerk of the Course acceded to the request. Typically, the Honda officials managed to get the engine stripped down away from the prying eyes of the press, who could only comment on how immaculate and free from oil the three machines appeared after racing at such frantic speeds. Significantly for Honda, eighteen of its much-loved production CR93 machines also completed the race, out of twenty that started it. Even though Honda had discontinued production of this model, they continued to be a mainstay of the 125cc event until it was dropped from the race calendar after 1974. Even then, some privateers had them re-engined to race in the 250cc TT.

A few hours after the 125cc Ultra-Lightweight came the 350cc Junior race. Unlike the 250cc class, here the Honda machine – the RC172 – was dominant and there was far less competition. Additionally Mike Hailwood, probably the biggest threat, had withdrawn his entry because he was ill with tonsillitis. The biggest challenge in his absence was likely to come from Alan Shepherd's 251cc MZ two-stroke. In an unusual move, Jim Redman was privately sponsoring a fellow countryman, Bruce Beale, on one of the previous year's 305cc Hondas, described as a 'semi-works' machine. Despite being twelve months old, the bike was still fast and capable of holding its own as it proved in practice (though Beale would only manage eleventh place in the race). Although originally down to start as number seventeen, Redman had obtained special dispensation to take over the number six allocated to Tommy Robb, a non-starter. Redman explained:

> Well it's a very small, light bike, and goes terrifically fast, which means it's quite lively on the roads but where the danger comes in … is not on the corners, where all the riders in the first twenty are graded and they're all good riders, but it's on the Isle of Man straights, which … are very fast 'kinks' rather than straights, and these other riders use all of the road as they are quite entitled to, and sort of cut across my bows as I'm coming up behind them. It happened a few times in practice, and that was

> the reason that made me go to the Stewards … My normal race tactics: start quickly and go as fast as you feel safe, and then rely on the signals to inform me of the position. Luigi [Taveri] is going out on another 350 so I can't afford to hang around or he'll be there, he's very quick … [16]

However, Taveri was also a non-starter, because just before it was to be weighed in, the Honda mechanics discovered an irreparable crack on the crank case of the second 350. Fearing that Redman's machine might have a similar problem, the team obtained special permission to check his engine after it had been weighed in, but all was well.

With the drop of the flag, Redman was fast from the start, taking the lead straight away and holding it through the race. He upped his pace on lap two and lap three, but found that he was simply racing the clock, as the opposition was so far behind. After pitting at the end of lap three he decided that engine preservation was the greatest priority. It was pointless racing to try to set a new lap record if it resulted in a blown engine and a DNF, so he eased off the pace on laps four, five and six, still winning comfortably. In fact, he was so far ahead of his nearest rivals that he had to wait around in the winner's enclosure for almost eight minutes before the next closest rider, Phil Read, came in. Redman had time to drink a can of Coca-Cola, chatted with friends, gave a TV interview, posed for photographers and even had a moment for a kiss from his proud wife Marlene. He commented afterwards:

> … The motorbike did all the work, I just sat on it. It's such a good bike, I just couldn't be off of winning on it, though possibly if Mike the Bike wasn't ill in bed I might have had to ride a lot harder [in the second half]. I suddenly remembered that if I didn't slow down, the boys wouldn't

> get their silvers [replicas], so I thought I'd better slow down! [laughter from other riders in background]. I'm sorry that Mike wasn't in the race because I would have liked to have beaten him if I could but as it was I can't complain, I had a nice easy ride.[17]

The 50cc event on the Friday of Race Week on the Isle of Man saw the return to the Manx roads of Naomi Taniguchi, who had not ridden on the Island since 1961. As already noted, regular Honda teamster Luigi Taveri had opted for Kreidler machinery for this race only, though he found the switch-over difficult, telling Murray Walker:

> The Kreidler is different from the Honda, its two stroke and its twelve speed, and the twelve speed is also different from the normal, because it is operated with the hand and with the foot, and for me it is very difficult to ride this bike.[18]

Hugh Anderson led the race from the start. After the first lap, the best Honda was that of Taniguchi in sixth place; second place was a battle between Kreidler and Suzuki, but as Bryans' new engine, freshly fitted just before the race, began to run in and loosen up, so he managed to carve his way through the field, from a starting position of seventh on lap one. By the final lap he was in a tussle with Morishita while lying third, but it was an outing utterly dominated by Anderson, who set a new lap record and new race record. Bryans managed a creditable second, and Taniguchi finished sixth. Honda's RC113, first introduced to the public at the previous year's end-of-season Japanese Grand Prix, featured a nine-speed gearbox and developed maximum power output at 18,500 rpm; the red line on the rev counter was set at

19,000 rpm, though it was permitted to go to 20,000 rpm if it was done briefly. The dry weight of the bike was 53kg, lower than its predecessor through the extensive use of magnesium, and a curious front brake. The latter was the same as that used on a normal bicycle, with two brake pads being clamped on to the rim. This saved total weight and unsprung weight, which improved handling. Two large, distinctive light alloy discs were mounted on the front wheel to give some streamlining. At the end of the 1964 TT Redman recalled:

> It will be a long time before I forget that week. To win one TT is a great achievement. To win two is a near miracle. And to have almost made it three on the run in the same week! Well, it's impossible to express my feelings … After the Junior race – the 350 – on Wednesday was over I relaxed for the first time. All the tensions, for me at last, were over for another year. I just put my feet up in my hotel, drank gallons of tea, and let myself unwind. I felt on top of the world.[19]

Yet he could not help thinking about Tom Phillis, his old friend without whose help he would never have become part of the Honda team. His consolation, however, was that he was awarded the MBE by Her Majesty Queen Elizabeth II for his services to motorcycle sport. It was one of his proudest achievements, even though such was the pace of the racing season that he was unable to find time to return to Salisbury to attend an investiture ceremony. Overall, Honda had much to be pleased about at the end of 1964. Redman took the 350cc world title with an emphatic performance – he won all eight rounds of the competition, and while Yamaha's Phil Read wrested the 250cc title away from Redman, there was a consolation in that Taveri took the 125cc title for Honda. Ralph

Bryans also managed second place in the 50cc championship behind Suzuki's Hugh Anderson. Soichiro Honda by now had achieved at least one of his ambitions, in that Honda Motor by 1964 were the largest motorcycle manufacturer in the world.

The following season, 1965, proved to be one of mixed results for Honda on the racetrack. The TT was preceded that year by rumours circulating in the British motorcycling press that Redman had been sensationally dropped by the Honda factory as one of their riders. It later transpired that the telegram that was supposedly the source of this story had not originated in Japan at all, it hadn't even come from overseas but instead had been 'concocted' in London. The GPO announced that they were making enquiries among their staff to discover a 'knowledgeable motorcyclist', presumably one also with a strange sense of humour. The irony was that this hoax was in complete contrast to the reality of the situation, with Honda in 1965 pouring massive resources into supporting Redman, almost to the detriment of their other riders. Top British racing journalist Mick Woollett, writing for *Motor Cycling*, was bemused by the whole situation, and summed it up in a report from the Island during Practice Week:

> Have Honda given up the fight to retain the 125cc World Championship won for them last year by Luigi Taveri? It certainly looks that way, for while two more 250cc machines were flown in from Japan – Redman now has a choice of four! – Luigi has waited in vain for the arrival of some new 125s. Honda brought with them to the Island the two four-cylinder bikes which have failed Taveri and Ralph Bryans in all three European World Championship rounds this year. Taveri's machine was out of action for much of Practice Week, so he and Ralph had to take it in turns to bash the lone surviving 125cc Honda around

> the Island. It seems incredible that Hondas, who spend such tremendous amounts on racing and research, should be letting this World Championship slip through their fingers while making frantic efforts to regain the 250cc title. Taveri is as baffled as everyone else – but what a frustrating situation for a World Champion riding for the world's richest motorcycle company to find himself in![20]

The racing schedule on the Island opened that year with the 250cc Lightweight race, and Honda entered only one of their new six-cylinder machines, to be ridden by Jim Redman. The 250cc 3RC164 engine was composed of two crankshafts, of three cylinders each, coupled in the centre of the engine. The cranks were reduced in weight by using tungsten components – stronger than steel – not as many suppose for the purpose of making the engine quicker revving (though it certainly was!) Rather, it was to increase the resonance frequency of the crank, at which it would begin to vibrate, away from the frequency of the firing engine. This would prevent or at least reduce the engine's tendency to self-destruct through internal vibration. One unintended consequence of this, however, was that it made the machine harder to ride; the low mass of the crank meant that it also had less momentum, and the engine had a tendency to stall when going into bends if the revs were not kept up by the rider. The general construction of the motor followed the usual Honda practice. Bore and stroke were 39 × 34.8 mm, for a total capacity of 249.43cc. Valve angle was 75 degrees, 34 degrees on the inlet and 41 degrees on the exhaust side. Spark plug size was the by now familiar 8mm. The ignition was by transistorised system – since 1964 the contact breaker method had been obsolete on Honda racers. Lubrication was by a wet sump system, but characteristically the engine would suffer from overheating problems. Mr Honda was convinced that air cooling was the simplest and most sensible approach with racing engines; water cooling might have solved these problems, but it was considered at the time that a water cooling system would be too heavy. Some years later the Honda company would eventually be forced to adopt this approach. The gearbox contained an eight-speed cluster. It produced 55bhp at 18,000 rpm, which was a 10 per cent increase on the previous year's four-cylinder 250. The engine was no wider than that of the RC161 four cylinder, but the bike used a larger fuel tank for the Isle of Man TT. Redman remembered that:

> The Honda 6 had first been discussed among riders and mechanics in 1964 but the fact that the machine was being developed in Japan was a closely guarded secret. Indeed, it was the best kept secret in racing when it had first appeared at Monza at the end of the [1964] season. The mechanics had taken two of the exhaust pipes off when it arrived to make it look more like a four-cylinder machine, and after the formidable array of pipes appeared at the race track, rival team members were falling over themselves to try to get a look. After each practice session it was quickly covered up with a blanket and kept under lock and key. So rushed however was its development that the engine had had only a few hours on a test bench. Much of the development work was done on the race track.[21]

Reporters had managed to grab a furtive photograph of the machine without its fairing at the French Grand Prix earlier in May, but that had merely served to whet the public appetite and now at the TT it seemed that everyone was out to get a snap of this elusive and rare beast. It was not just the sight but the sound of the Honda six that caused excitement among the race-going public in the paddock. The sound when the Honda mechanics revved them as they warmed up has been likened to a dog bark, a short aggressive 'whoop-whoop-whoop' that ended the moment the throttle was released. Redman, however, had other concerns; he urgently needed a win in this race, because he was still yet to score a single point in that year's 250cc World Championship, while rival Phil Read had already won four rounds. Redman told Murray Walker before the race:

> Of course it's much quicker than the four … I don't think it handles quite as well, but I think I've got it handling fairly well now, and I'm quite happy with it. It's very quick, and of course … it has a very narrow powerband, so it's more difficult to ride, especially at places like Governor's Bridge and Ramsey Hairpin, very difficult. 17,000 rpm is where they put the red line … I think going down to the Highlander is probably about the quickest on the 250, and I'd say it's a speed of about 145 or so. It's fairly obvious that Phil Read is the man to beat. Phil likes the Isle of Man, he's always been very fast here, so I don't feel as confident as I would perhaps at another circuit on the continent, but also its a long circuit and a long race, and a lot can happen, as last year when I was a rank outsider.[22]

Setting off as number two, Redman was in the lead at Barregarrow on the first lap, being chased hard by Phil Read on the Yamaha. By the Grandstand he had taken the lead, smashing the lap record in the process. Two miles later at Quarter Bridge Redman was still first on the road, but Read was right behind him. Satellite rider Bruce Beale was riding a Honda four and putting in a fine performance. By the Gooseneck on lap two Read had passed Redman and was five seconds ahead on the road – twenty-five seconds in the lead on corrected time. However, it was not to last. Only 2 miles further on Read suffered a broken crankpin, and was forced to retire. By lap three Redman had a thirty-five-second advantage over next-placed man Bill Ivy. By lap four the weather was deteriorating, and with heavy mist on the Mountain, Bill Ivy came off at Brandywell. Redman was left with a lead of nearly two minutes by the start of the fifth lap. By the final circuit Beale was holding station in sixth place, and looked assured of finishing in that position until, agonisingly close to the end, he ran out of fuel. Redman, by contrast, never put a foot wrong. He made history by becoming the first rider to win three 250cc TTs in succession. After the flag Redman described his epic battle with Read in the early part of the race:

> I didn't have any signals on the first lap until I got to Governor's Bridge, and I got a signal '-15 Phil' which I knew meant +5 on the road and I knew that he could see me. I went down to Ballacraine on the second lap and had a look around and I could see him just coming round the corner and I reckoned I had about three seconds lead on him there. I knew he must be closing the gap, and I had the uncanny feeling in the back of my neck that he was right there for some time, but I don't like to look back and then after Rhencullen on the very fast section to Ballaugh Bridge I saw his front wheel come alongside once, and then eventually down towards Ballaugh he did get through, and from there I never headed him again. He stayed in front and I did my best to keep up with him, but I was losing ground – slightly, but losing. I planned to stay with him, and if he had given me an opportunity

> I would have gone through, because if you are in front you can do exactly what you want to do, and if you are behind you sometimes have to shut off when you don't want to, and those two strokes, the more they shut off and turn on again, the more likely they are to give trouble. So I tried to keep up with Phil, hoping I'd get a chance to slip through and maybe slow him up on a slow section and maybe oil a plug for him! He went away from me steadily, and I think he must have had about three seconds' lead when the bike seized. I could see him, we were going up the Mountain Mile at the time, and we got about three quarters of the way up there, and I suddenly saw Phil sit up and grab the clutch and I thought, 'You beauty, she's blown!'[23]

In the 125cc class the team started the season with the previous year's 2RC146; they retired in West Germany and Spain and ended up down the field in France. On the Isle of Man, on the Wednesday morning of Race Week, the upgraded 4RC146 made its competitive debut. Taveri came in second in the Ultra-Lightweight TT, the best place of the season. The 4RC146 was an improved version of the 2RC146, and nearly identical to it – the only external difference was the shorter exhausts of the 4RC146. Power output was now 30bhp at 17,000 rpm. In actual practice, however, the engine hardly ever ran well, with continual carburation and ignition problems. For the preceding four years the Ultra-Lightweight TT had been something of a grudge match between Honda and Suzuki, with the honours shared evenly between them. Now it was to be a three-way battle, as for the first time Yamaha entered a team of three riders: Read, Ivy and Canadian Mike Duff. Suzuki rider Hugh Anderson was frank when he admitted he expected more problems from these machines than from the Hondas, because of the difficulties that the latter team had been having with their 125 machines. Luigi Taveri gave his honest assessment of what the chances of his motorcycle were:

> I think the Honda is always OK and will make easily the three laps, only this year with a little more trouble; I think it is carburetor trouble and ignition. I don't know if I can go faster [than last year] or not, but sure if it's a good day Yamaha or Suzuki can go faster. The Honda cannot beat the Suzuki, as the speed at the moment is not the same as the Suzuki; for Yamaha it will be a little more difficult for them to finish the race.[24]

At Kirk Michael, 14 miles out, Taveri was leading on the road, with Read in pursuit. No. 19 Ralph Bryans was late at Kirk Michael, though there was nothing obviously wrong with his Honda. At the end of the first lap Taveri passed the Grandstand with Read right behind him. The English rider caught the Swiss maestro at Brandywell and on the last lap the pair went through Quarter Bridge together (although Read was by this point twenty seconds ahead on corrected time). Bryans was holding steady in sixth place. Luigi describes the final stages of the race, and the battle with Read's Yamaha, which was now having problems of its own, as the pressure began to make itself felt on the machinery:

> At the Tourist Trophy I proved to myself that I could still ride motorcycles. Phil Read had gone into the race thirty seconds after me. When he caught up with me in the second lap, there was a good opportunity to draw a stark comparison of our machines. Read was much faster on the straight. I remained in position several miles behind him. Then his lead grew bigger. In the last circuit I suddenly saw him in front of me. I came closer and closer, and at

> Signpost Corner I even managed to overtake, a mile before the chequered flag. After I had run over the line, it took a long time for Read to get there. Had I managed to win? No, Phil's time was better than mine by four seconds, although his machine had only run on one cylinder in the last few miles![25]

As well as winning the 250cc race, Redman also did well in the 350cc Junior TT, also on the Wednesday of Race Week, despite encountering problems almost everywhere else this season. The biggest threat was from MV Agusta's new 350cc triple, which in the hands of Giacomo Agostini (making his TT debut) had just beaten Redman's Honda in the West German Grand Prix. Redman had this to say about the new Italian machine:

> Well, having been beaten by it, I have to say it's very good! But I must add that the Honda did break a camshaft in West Germany and we'd thrown the engine together – a remarkable job having to strip the engine, strip an old four-cylinder 250 and rob the camshaft and rebuild it into the 350 within a couple of hours between practice and the race, and the bike wasn't up to Honda's normal standards. So I can't really tell how much my bike was off to get a good indication of the speed of the MV, but I do know that my bike, having been sent back to Japan and rebuilt there, it's going perfectly, and I think we'll have as good a chance as anyone else![26]

At 1.30pm in perfect weather conditions the race got under way. The Honda proved itself to be incredibly fast. By Kirk Michael, Redman had made up fourteen seconds to catch Agostini on the road, but by Brandish, almost at the end of the first lap, Hailwood on the other MV was catching Redman. By the end of this lap the order on the road was Redman, Hailwood, Agostini, with the Englishman leading the race by twenty seconds on corrected time. However, Hailwood soon seemed in trouble with oil observed soaking his leg as he passed the Grandstand. Pressing on undaunted, he and Redman were wheel to wheel, riding as a pair throughout lap two. By lap three, in spite of a stretched chain that was jumping the sprockets, Hailwood was leading Redman by half a minute and had only to keep him in sight in order to win. Bruce Beale was holding sixth place at this point on his Honda four, riding through the pain barrier with a fractured thumb. Adding to the tension, the two leaders came into the pits together. Italian mechanics could be seen frantically wiping oil from their machine. More concerning was the problem with the rear sprocket, and vital seconds ticked by as the mechanics struggled to adjust the chain. Redman, meanwhile, was already away and the Grandstand pubic address announced that he had retaken the lead. Agostini entered the MV pits while Hailwood's machine was still receiving attention, creating further confusion and delaying him also.

By the middle of lap four Redman was out on his own. The MV problems had promoted Phil Read on his 254cc Yamaha to second place both on the road and the race. But it was Redman's race to lose from this point onward and the sure-footed Rhodesian knew the Honda's reliability was his secret weapon. He repeated his feat of earlier in the week, in becoming the first rider to win three Junior TT races in succession. Asked by journalists afterwards if he had had any problems, Redman commented:

> Only Mike Hailwood! I think that the Honda was quicker, but Mike was riding harder. I didn't realise that Mike

> hadn't restarted [after the pit stop] with me until I looked back at the top of the hill out of Union Mills. I couldn't see Mike and I thought, 'You beauty, I may be able to get away from him.' At Ramsey I got a signal telling me that I was two minutes ahead and I knew that Mike must be in real trouble.[27]

After that, he explained, he had begun to worry if he would have enough petrol to finish the race; his pit stop, at 19.4 seconds, had been so quick that he was afraid he might not have taken on enough fuel. With Hailwood out, Redman decided to refuel again after five laps. He actually had the filler cap open, and was about to come in when he decided that Read was too close, and abandoned the idea. He need not have worried, however – the lateral-thinking Japanese mechanics had measured the amount of fuel that was left in the quick filler, in order to work out exactly how much Jim had taken on board, and knew that he was safe. At the end of the race Redman's machine appeared rather battered, with one megaphone broken and the other chipped.

In the 50cc races Honda did very well that year with the RC115, winning five of the eight World Championship rounds including that at the TT, and Taveri again takes up the story from the Isle of Man:

> The 50cc race took place two days later – in fearful weather. My Honda left the start line only on a single cylinder. I had already resigned myself to the fact that the race was lost and wanted to give up on the first lap. On the long straight to Union Mills, however, the awkward cylinder suddenly started again. Now the machine ran on full power once more. But did it make sense to continue the hopeless race? Rain lashed towards us all over the

> course, whilst wind and fog made the journey dangerous. The light racing machines (they weigh only about 50kg) are of course particularly exposed to gusts when they are driven at full speed.
>
> I got into a gust several times and was 'offset' up to two metres, a game ball in the hands of the weather. It is something else to be thrown from one side of the road to the other, not only trying to stay in control on the corners, but also judge the (unpredictable) gusts of wind correctly and to not even have a clear view ahead. At the end of the first lap around the circuit it was indicated to me that I was second. How was that possible? What had happened? In any case, all my thoughts were blown away. A lap later I was even in the top position. Apparently I had covered the 'Mountain' faster in the fog than the Japanese rider Itoh, who had come over it prior to me. This commanding position was now not going to be lost. Not that I would have driven safely now. Tenths of a second are even more important than usual in a TT where you don't have an overview of the race.
>
> And it worked! I was allowed to stand on the middle podium at the award ceremony, Anderson (as second placed) to my right, Degner to the left; Itoh was pushed out of the top three. In the World Championship standings I had put myself between the New Zealander and the East German. The weather had – as I learned at the chequered flag – given even more trouble to my opponents than to me. Bryans had found it so difficult that he preferred to give up.[28]

The RC115 had a completely new engine. Drive to the camshafts was still with a gear train on the right-hand side, but was now taken from the clutch drive instead of from a gear on the crankshaft. Also the megaphones were not welded to the down pipes as usual for Hondas, but slipped over them – necessitated by the fact that they were made of aluminium, in order to save weight. The carburetors had flat slides. Power output was a healthy 15bhp at 20,000 rpm, and lubrication was by wet sump; there were nine speeds in the gearbox. The dry weight as noted by Taveri was 50kg – compared with the 61kg of the single-cylinder CR110 offered to privateers. During the season, both high-level exhausts and the normal low-level exhausts were used. The high-level exhausts had the advantage of a smaller frontal area, because the fairing could be kept narrower, which gave less air drag. Bryans, in spite of his retirement at the TT, became the 1965 50cc World Champion, with Taveri second. Honda took the manufacturer's title in this class.

By this point, Honda's thoughts were turning to the 500c class, the only solo category that thus far they had not contested. So far, their motorcycle was still at the design stage, so for the 1965 Senior TT they decided to enter Redman on a 450cc machine, which in fact housed a bored-out 350cc engine. As usual there was much cloak-and-dagger secrecy from Honda and the machine was entered into the race by the Rhodesian Motor Sports Association in order to obscure its true origins. At the last minute, Honda got cold feet and pulled out, fearing that the machine could suffer an embarrassing defeat. Redman told *Motor Cycle News*:

> This particular machine is my idea and was first thought of last year. I discussed it with the designer, knowing the potential of the existing 350, and he has taken it from there … It is just awaiting assembly in Japan, but with all the work to prepare machines for the other classes, 50, 125, 250 and 350 – plus the new racing cars, it couldn't

> be put together in time and tested as well ... It is meant just for me, and the Isle of Man TT is just about the only place where we could use it. I am prevented from using it anywhere else in this season's Classics by the FIM distance limit of racing miles than can be covered by any one rider in a day.[29]

Honda's 1965 season resulted in two riders' World Championships and two manufacturer's Championships, at 350cc and 50cc levels, but their ambition was to be successful across the board. This would lead them in the coming season to contest the 500cc class – the blue riband of motorcycle racing – with the same determination and competitiveness with which they had first tackled the smaller classes. If anything, the racing would be even closer, the thrills and dices even more spectacular. The Isle of Man would be the stage for some of the greatest of these 500cc clashes in the next two years.

Chapter Five

1966–67
TAMING THE BEAST

Opinion differs on exactly how and why Mike Hailwood became a Honda factory rider in 1966. Some sources state that he left MV Agusta in disgust when he learned that he would be second rider in the team behind Giacomo Agostini, adding that he tore his contract up in front of Count Agusta. Hailwood's own memoir paints things slightly differently, with Mike stating that towards the end of 1964 things were going badly for him in terms of his racing career. Although he was dominating everything on his 500 MV, he was finding this class boring as there was so little competition. By contrast, in the 350cc class, he was growing deeply frustrated by the fact that MV's machine was simply not up to the task and he was continually being beaten by Redman's Honda. Hailwood pestered the Count to make improvements to the 350, but he was not interested, seeing only the success that the 500 model was bringing. At last the Count relented and agreed to work on the smaller-capacity engine, but nothing came of it. Hailwood was by now making overtures towards Honda, but despite the efforts of Redman on his behalf, he was rebuffed. He admitted that he was more upset than he let on by the rejection, and even though he was wooed by Suzuki, he was put off by their two strokes (in particular, their tendency to seize and throw off the rider) so he stuck with MV, reasoning that if nothing else, it was easy money; he signed a new contract with Count Agusta at the start of 1965. In the meantime. Honda had invited Alan Shepherd to ride for them, so Hailwood looked even more out of favour. That is, until Shepherd was injured. Mike takes up the story:

> One morning towards the end of '65, shortly before the Japanese Grand Prix, when the usual heap of mail dropped through my letterbox, tucked away in the middle of it all was a letter with a Japanese stamp on it. It was from Honda. I looked at it for ages without thinking about opening it; I tried to find a dozen reasons why they should be writing to me, without even considering the obvious one. When I opened it, it said:
>
> Dear Sir,
> I congratulate you bring about good results. Now as in my opinion, I hope reply whether you are will ride in Honda 6 (250cc) at '65 Japan GP race or not. I recommend in an instant for Honda Motor Co, Ltd. I await reply.
>
> It was signed by H. Sekiguchi, the director of Research and Development at Honda. His grammar may have been shaky, but the message was plain.
>
> The main thing about Honda was that you could always rely on them to dig out something special when it was needed. It made the prospect of riding for them extremely attractive. To my mind they were the tops in the business, way ahead of the field. There wasn't a rider in the world who'd have turned down a chance to race for them.
>
> I suppose that when I first wanted to join them my enthusiasm came at an inopportune time. I would have been a luxury they could well have done without; they were doing quite nicely without needing to strengthen their line-up. Jim was winning everything in sight on the

> 250 and 350, and the 500 was still a few sketchy lines on the drawing-boards.[1]

In Hailwood's memoir he states that Count Agusta allowed him to go to Japan to try out the machine, and the British motorcycle press was already awash with rumours that Honda was about to sign him up (it would transpire that they were right on this point, but rather wide of the mark in their other claim that the Japanese firm was also looking to sign up South African Paddy Driver as a support rider). Mike refused to comment on the speculation, but it was Stan Hailwood who really let the cat out of the bag when he told *Motor Cycling*:

> Mike wants more rides. He doesn't get enough to keep in practice. He also wants to do more racing in England and we can't seem to rely on getting the MVs. This means that we have to borrow bikes and depend on the kindness of other people – which isn't fair to them or, because he doesn't know the bikes, to Mike.[2]

In spite of its difficult handling, he won the end of season 250cc Japanese Grand Prix on the six-cylinder machine, as well as taking victory in the 350cc class, and on the strength of this performance Honda offered him a contract for 1966, which he signed. Mike revealed that there was no haggling over cash; he suggested a sum and they agreed to it right away – rumour had it among the fans that it was £40,000 per year, more than half a million pounds in today's terms. For Hailwood though it was also the realisation of an ambition that he had held for more than two years:

> [Honda] backed their racing effort with an investment previously unheard of in the bike world. Undisclosed

> sums went into research, organisation and back-up services. They flooded the circuits with factory 'specials' and handed out fat contracts to the riders they decided should make up their team. Because of Honda's blind obsession with racing domination they paid well, and works riders, perhaps for the first time, were able to claim the right money for risking their necks racing. Not that Honda were a pushover. It wasn't easy to get a Honda works ride – even in their most active years – and like most factories they often wanted a lot without paying enough for it. They were sometimes unreasonable, unpredictable, stubborn and ruthless. But they hoisted motor cycling out of its 'cloth-cap' image, gave it sparkle and sophistication, and made international, jet-set heroes of their racing stars.[3]

Becoming for the first time a full member of the Honda team, Hailwood found a new respect for Jim Redman. He wrote later:

> In the light of their history of atrocious handling, Jim Redman comes out as a far better rider than most people are prepared to give him credit for. To my mind he's twice as good as anybody ever rated him; he deserved every one of his titles. Nobody would have had to work harder for them than he did.[4]

The fact was that Redman had been riding Hondas for years by this point and never complained about the handling; he accepted it as part of the deal. He had wanted to be a works rider and new, unproven machines straight from the factory race shop were part and parcel of the deal. To have complained about it was not in Redman's style, he would have considered it ungrateful, or disloyal (and would also have been acutely aware that there were many other riders who would have taken his place in a heartbeat).

While in Japan Mike tried out the prototype 500cc machine that Honda were developing. The problems inherent in it showed themselves right away. While the MV equivalent was docile, the Honda handled very badly. Hailwood suggested some improvements, which the firm agreed to, but shortly after he joined the team it was decided that Redman should concentrate on the big bike class, while Hailwood tackled the 250cc and 350cc categories, so Mike reasoned that it was no longer his problem anyway. He would only be a support rider in the bigger class. Whatever the difficulties the Honda 500 presented, it was still good enough to beat the 1965 MV rival, which was something like 25 per cent down on horsepower in comparison. However, the Japanese firm, who usually set so much store by secrecy, made a rare misstep by announcing publicly that they would be unveiling a 100bhp 500cc machine for the 1966 season. Count Agusta sat up and took notice, and duly began improvements to his own machine that brought it to within 2mph of the Honda's top speed. Given the previously mentioned superior handling of the MV, it was now going to be a very difficult package to beat, especially in the hands of a rider as good as Giacomo Agostini. The main weakness of the MV lay in the fact that, unlike the Honda, over-revving it was fatal. Anything over 10,800 rpm would bend the valves and blow the pistons, so the rider had to pay very close attention to the needle on the rev counter. The Honda was much more forgiving in this regard.

The 1966 TT unusually was held in August and September, as a National Union of Seamen strike in June forced its postponement, and the ships of the Isle of Man Steam Packet

Company were tied up in harbour all summer. There was much debate that year about whether a TT would actually take place, and if it did would it count for World Championship points. Things were finally resolved when Honda confirmed that they would attend the postponed races; by now acknowledged as the strongest racing team in the world, if they attended then the other manufacturers were bound to follow suit. Even when the situation returned to normal, however, the Honda squad faced a problem when race bikes being shipped from Amsterdam were delayed at Liverpool airport by a mix-up. This meant that the team was late starting practice. Further bad luck followed. Mike Hailwood blew the motor on a six, and a 125 being used by Ralph Bryans caught fire and was destroyed, Bryans revealing:

> I was coming along past the eleventh milestone and found the machine wasn't going as quick as it normally did when I accelerated out of the bends. I changed down some gears and rode along for another mile and this wasn't getting any better. I thought something's gone wrong, so I looked down and there were flames licking around the carburettors so I thought well if I lift the clutch and rev the engine maybe it'll suck the flames down into the cylinders, and it'll go out, so I tried that and it didn't go out, so I thought well if I go faster it'll maybe blow the flames so I went faster, and I looked down and it was still getting worse so I eventually arrived at the thirteenth milestone and it must have burnt through one of the petrol pipes because there was an almighty blaze, so I just jumped off, dropped it and ran for my life![5]

During early morning practice on the Wednesday, Hailwood missed a gear, which on a wet road saw him slide off his machine at Braddan. The following day, however, it seemed that the jinxes were behind him, as he unofficially broke Redman's Lightweight TT lap record. Ralph Bryans did something similar in the 50cc class.

The 1966 event also saw the last appearance of Jim Redman as a Honda rider. Having crashed badly earlier in the season in pouring rain at the Belgian Grand Prix, he struggled on but found he was not fit enough to start a race. After discussions with Honda management during Practice Week, Redman, a man admired more than liked, who was sometimes described as unapproachable, uncommunicative, and unemotional, announced his retirement from Grand Prix racing. His was a towering achievement – his tally of six TT wins and an MBE hardly beginning to reflect the impact that he made on motorcycle sport. He told reporters:

> I had it in mind to pack it in at the end of the year if I could win the 500cc World Championship. But my broken arm put paid to that, and I nearly changed my mind so that I could try again next year. Still, you can go on forever like that, so I decided to make the break now. However, I'm under contract to Honda until after the Japanese Grand Prix in October, so I had to speak to them about it before I could confirm my intentions. Now I have spoken to Mr Sekiguchi, head of Honda's racing department, who has come over for the TT, and he has suggested that this would be a good time to announce my retirement.

When it was suggested that he might become a non-riding team manager for Honda he replied:

> I haven't been offered the job and even if I had, I don't know whether I would take it. I've had a number of offers, but I haven't made up my mind yet what to do.[6]

It was a particularly serious blow for Honda because it had been envisaged that Redman would concentrate on the 500cc class that season, while Hailwood targeted the smaller classes. Now Hailwood also had to pick up the reins on the 500cc machine mid-season, with half of the World Championship races already gone. In an effort to assist him, Honda recruited Stuart Graham, but he only made one appearance for the firm at the TT that year in the Lightweight race, in which he finished second.

Unusually, the 250cc Lightweight TT was held on the Sunday prior to Race Week, and the race saw a virtuoso performance by Hailwood. After a relaxed start when he coolly adjusted his leathers as he pulled away from the line, it seemed at first that there would be few fireworks, but then he tore into his rivals with a blistering first lap that put the record up by an astonishing 4mph. His only real rival, Phil Read, retired at Ginger Hall on the second lap with a broken crankshaft. Hailwood made a faultless pit stop at the end of the third lap with the Honda six sounding sweeter than ever. However, teammate Stuart Graham had a nightmare moment when he made a hash of his refuelling session. He struggled for over two precious minutes to restart his machine after he failed to sufficiently flood his carburetors. The only saving grace was that Yamaha rival Bill Ivy made an equally serious mistake when he overshot his pit. With his engine misfiring, he also had to change plugs, which meant that Graham was still able to secure second place. Afterwards Hailwood commented:

> It was a bit boring. I was only revving to 17,000 rpm (normally it is 18,000 rpm) when chasing Phil on the first lap, then I knocked it off to 16,500.[7]

Right: Mrs Keiko Carran, who assisted the Japanese speaking riders in the early years at the TT. (Courtesy of Manx National Heritage)

Below: The 1959 Honda team, photographed behind the TT grandstand before heading home. (Courtesy of TT Racepics)

Bottom: Hailwood's 1961 125cc machine, which scored Honda's first TT win. (Author's Collection)

Above: Jim Redman (Honda) looks across at Mike Hailwood (MV) at the start of the 1963 Junior TT. Redman won this race, which was run in less than ideal conditions. (Courtesy of Ken Sprayson)

Below: Kunimitsu Takahashi in the 1963 Ultra-Lightweight TT. He finished 8th in this race. (TT Racepics)

Right: Tommy Robb, on the start line for the 1963 Lightweight TT, which took place in sweltering conditions. The trademark white gloves of the Honda mechanics were not, as many suppose, to keep the machinery clean, but were instead worn to prevent burns from hot engine parts. (Courtesy of Ken Sprayson)

Below: Naomi Taniguchi before the 1964 50cc TT race. Note the wide aluminium disc on the front wheel which was characteristic of the RC113 machine. (TT Racepics)

Above: Luigi Taveri (Honda) races Hugh Anderson (Suzuki) away from the line in the 1964 Ultra Lightweight TT race. (Courtesy of Ken Sprayson)

Below left: Luigi Taveri at the start of the 1964 Lightweight TT. Note the mechanic's jacket, covering the engine to conceal it as much as possible from the eyes (and cameras) of rival firms. (Courtesy of Ken Sprayson)

Below right: Jim Redman warming up the 250cc Honda 6 for the 1965 Lightweight TT. (Courtesy of Ken Sprayson)

Stuart Graham in the 1966 Lightweight TT. Note the distinctive triple exhaust pipes of the six cylinder engine. (Courtesy of Ranscombe Photographic)

Above: Mike Hailwood in the 1966 Lightweight TT. The race was held in the cooler conditions of September this year. (Courtesy of Ken Sprayson)

Below left: Hailwood's winner's sash from the 1966 Senior TT. In this era, the colour of the sash reflected that of the number plate used for that class - yellow was for the Senior. (Courtesy of Manx National Heritage)

Below right: A Honda mechanic's cap, given away to a young fan at the Grandstand. (Courtesy of Manx National Heritage)

Above: Start of the 1967 Lightweight TT. Ralph Bryans looks across at the MZ of Derek Woodman. Mike Hailwood is behind him with number 7. (Courtesy of Ken Sprayson)

Below left: Prior to the start of the 1967 Junior TT – Hailwood looks on whilst the grey-overalled Honda mechanics work their magic. (Courtesy of Ken Sprayson)

Below right: Hailwood calmly awaits the start of the 1967 Junior TT. (Courtesy of Ken Sprayson)

Above: Hailwood on the Mountain in the 1967 Junior TT, banking the six cylinder machine slightly to reveal the gap in the fairing, allowing maximum passage of air. (Courtesy of Ken Sprayson)

Below: Hailwood in the 1967 Senior TT, aboard the mighty 500cc Honda. It was a difficult machine to handle and only a rider of Hailwood's calibre could have done it. (Courtesy of Ken Sprayson)

Left: A Honda supporter's T-shirt from the TT races of the mid-60s. Merchandising was in its infancy at this time, so a local firm came up with this design which Honda approved and allowed them to use. (Author's collection)

Below: The 1961 Hailwood 250cc machine, winner of that year's Lightweight TT and now owned by the National Motor Museum, Beaulieu. Without the usual fairing, details of the engine are revealed. (Courtesy of John Dalton)

Ever the comedian, Hailwood joked that if he had gone any slower then the machine would have toppled over. His Honda completed the race in good order with no obvious oil leakage, the only signs of stress being a worn back tyre and a very slack chain. Due to the cooler weather at this time of year there were hardly any flies splattered on the fairing, as one might have expected in June. At the end of the 1966 season, Graham left for Suzuki. However, he retained fond memories of his time with Honda, commenting:

> The Honda 6 was by far the quickest thing I'd ridden on the Isle of Man. I had a couple of practice laps on an old machine I'd ridden in the Ulster Grand Prix, but then a new one was shipped over for me, with better handling. Even so, I managed to have a heart-stopping moment at Laurel Bank when the back stepped out. I semi-high-sided and brushed a wall with my left boot, then shot across the road and mounted the pavement. I managed to stay in control somehow and carry on. In the race, my job was to back up Mike [Hailwood] and not take risks, bringing the bike home safely … With hindsight I could wish that I had gone a bit harder but that race really boosted my confidence. After all, I had been thrust into the premier factory team halfway through my first GP season. By the next round in Italy I had really got the hang of the six.[8]

The Wednesday morning 125cc race was considered by tipsters to be too close to call; many thought that championship leader Taveri was the favourite but the re-entry of Hailwood into this class as a Honda teamster introduced an element of doubt. However, the race saw Honda, usually so sure-footed, take an uncharacteristic beating from arch-rivals Yamaha. In this event

Honda fielded the new five-cylinder RC149. The previous year's four-cylinder 125cc machine was by this stage clearly outclassed, and the factory racing department responded by multiplying the championship-winning 50cc twin engine by two and a half. The problem of what to do with the exhaust pipe from the fifth cylinder was solved by hoisting it over the cam boxes and taking it out under the seat – an arrangement that must have been uncomfortable for the rider! The crankshaft had a special configuration: the three-cylinder part had the crankpins at 120 degrees, the two-cylinder part had the crankpins, in the usual Honda fashion, at 180 degrees. Both crankshafts were coupled together at the position of the camshaft drive.

The valve angle was 56 degrees, 24 degrees for the inlet and 32 degrees for the exhaust valves. The lubrication system was by wet sump, with two oil coolers in the sides of the fairing. There was also an oil temperature gauge. The oil temperature was checked, and the coolers could be covered more or less to maintain the oil temperature within certain limits. Power output was 38bhp at 20,500 rpm, which was less than might be expected, but the complicated crankshaft arrangement reduced the mechanical efficiency to a certain extent. The polyester petrol tank unusually had an unpainted strip, to allow the petrol level to be checked visually. Luigi Taveri was impressed by it, but admitted it had drawbacks:

> The five cylinder is a very nice bike and sure the bike is faster than the four cylinder only the difference is this new bike is much more difficult for riding.[9]

Bryans also had his reservations:

> Being lighter and faster it leaps about the road a lot more than the old four cylinder did. It's very, very difficult to

> bring out of slow corners because it pops and splutters and bangs. It does everything but want to go. It only runs at very high revolutions.[10]

Carburation problems hampered Mike Hailwood's efforts on the Honda five, but he was still the best placed of the team at the end of lap one, in sixth place. The Honda machines had been set up for cool and damp conditions but the race was delayed and by the time it started the weather was warm and dry. All the team's riders experienced difficulties with over-jetting as a result. Luigi Taveri had caused further problems for himself at Ballacraine by running off the track, costing him valuable seconds, while Yamaha's Bill Ivy was having the race of his life. Teammate and arch-rival Phil Read had been the early race leader but Ivy overhauled him – not through any benevolence from Read, however, as Ivy posted a lap of 98.55mph, a phenomenal speed for a 125cc machine. Taveri's problems continued and at the end of lap two he pulled into the pits. The mechanics literally turned the machine upside down in an attempt to cure its ailments. He spent more than two minutes in the pit lane while two of the plugs were changed, and then the machine had to be tilted on to its back wheel to clear the flooded combustion chambers. Both he and Ralph Bryans continued to have carburation problems and Hailwood passed them both on the road, despite shaking his head in despair at his mechanics to indicate that all was not well with his own mount. Hailwood's sixth place was Honda's best finish in this race. Luigi Taveri finished eighth, and remembered:

> Honda decided to also put Mike Hailwood on the 125. But none of our machines ran properly. In practice, Bill Ivy (Yamaha) had given nothing away and always kept

> his true form hidden. He started the race twenty seconds behind. When he overtook me, I wanted to follow him. I had to look twice as he almost accidentally crashed. He had stretched his arms and legs out from himself, and it is a mystery to me how he always stayed on the machine and on the track. I was afraid for him and feared the worst. But finally the winner was still named as Bill Ivy. Hailwood finished fifth as the best Honda rider. This race was discussed for a long time. Ivy later told me: 'If I think about what I did back then, I still get goose bumps.' Bill was a step closer to the World Championship ranking.[11]

In the Junior TT on the Wednesday afternoon of Race Week, Hailwood had hopes of coming within reach of the great Stanley Woods' tally of ten TT wins. Talking about his prospects before the race, he mused:

> The Honda is probably a little better all round than the MV three, it certainly handles better than the MV I rode last year, but they seem to have got that sorted out. They've obviously developed the engine more during the winter, if anything its generally better than the 350 Honda. The poor old thing's a bit obsolete now, they're going to have to bring out something new … I'd like to see more horsepower![12]

Hailwood set off like a missile when the flag dropped, setting a blistering pace. However, his dreams were dashed within ten minutes of the start, when he was reported to be out of the race at Bishopscourt with a broken magneto. This was not the full story, for it later transpired that his 350cc machine had dropped four of its eight exhaust valves into the two right-hand cylinders, destroying the engine. When they were examined after the race, it was found that these new valves, sent from Japan specially for the TT, were all faulty. When the others were tested, they were found to be brittle and snapped as easily as a raw carrot. The failure gifted the win to rival Agostini, who was a favourite even before Hailwood's mishap.

In the 50cc race Ralph Bryans scored a record-breaking win against a much-depleted field of only seventeen starters, down from an original poor entry of twenty-nine. It was the first time a massed start had been employed for this event but there were too few entrants for it to be particularly exciting. Taveri noted:

> At the Tourist Trophy, my 50cc machine did not run the way it should. We had the opportunity to test our machines at a military airfield. With the 'problem child' we made days of attempts. After the last practice session, she ran, but she didn't give her best performance. I already had two victories in this class, Bryans none yet. For me, the World Championship was within reach, because I was in the lead in front of Hans-Georg Anscheidt and would have taken the title with a TT victory. Ralph, on the other hand, had practically no chance of the world title. I suggested that we should exchange the machines. But the team leadership would not allow it.
>
> 50cc is the only class that is at the Tourist Trophy in which riders set off with a mass start. Bryans and I immediately took the lead until Ramsey Hairpin was before us. But then my difficulties started. At a sharp bend, the eye deceived me for several seconds. I struggled to catch up with this gap. With the first lap completed, I was only four seconds behind Bryans. But it's not easy to overtake a Ralph Bryans who is really a specialist in the smallest class. Of course, he also saw his chance and

> drove with the maximum when the distance had become a little bigger again. Bryans won and now, contrary to all the expectations, was in with a chance of winning his second world championship title.[13]

Bryans took the lead from the start, never to lose it, with Taveri in second place. His RC116, however, was an incredible machine, and serves to highlight just how advanced four-stroke technology was sixty years ago. Indeed, this was the most advanced of all the Honda engines used at the TT. The red line was at 22,500 rpm, and power output was 16bhp at 21,500 rpm, which equates to 320bhp per litre – a figure that has never been surpassed by any naturally aspirated four-stroke engine since. With a gearbox containing a nine-speed cluster, this was a formidable machine.

The two Hondas quickly shook off their Suzuki rivals and roared away, showing they were in a class of their own. Only the last lap brought some worries to the Honda camp, as Bryans' twin-cylinder engine began to cut and splutter, dropping to one pot at Creg ny Baa with only about 4 miles to go. This, his only real difficulty, was caused by a loose plug lead, but he was able to push it back on while still riding. A mile further on at Brandish the offending cylinder burst back into life for him to win by 51.2 seconds. Sixth-placed Dave Simmonds, though on a privately entered machine, was named as the third member of the team by Honda, thus giving them the manufacturer's team prize for this event. The middle order among the finishers was dominated by Honda's off the shelf 50cc racing machine, the CR110. Yet it had been out of production by two years at this point and was becoming difficult to get hold of, so consequently it commanded a high price on the second-hand market. This was due to the fact that the model had virtually assured reliability. In the hands of a competent rider it only had to start a race to become the hot favourite, and it dominated the 50cc class outside of World Championship racing. With 8.5 bhp at 13,500 rpm, it produced around 25 per cent more power than the Italian two strokes of the same capacity that formed its main opposition. The single-cylinder engine featured two overhead camshafts and four valves with an eight-speed gearbox. The riding experience was described as being like no other. The machine slipped and slid into corners in a way that could catch out the unwary rider; a fast '50' drifting was said to be like riding on hard sand – the rider never being quite sure how far it would go, and a racing line could not be plotted with the same precision as was possible on a larger motorcycle. This was a machine that could almost guarantee a leader board position – but first you had to learn how to ride it!

Nevertheless, this class was already coming in for criticism at World Championship level as a two-horse race, and Honda pulled out of 50cc and 125cc racing at the end of the 1966 season. This was to be Taveri's final competitive appearance at the TT. He remembered:

> Honda sent me a contract for 1967 shortly after the end of the season. I never signed it, I couldn't make up my mind. They wrote to me from Japan several times. The Japanese did not want to lose a top driver after Redman's resignation. But I no longer felt the slightest enthusiasm for racing. I discussed it with my wife several times, but I couldn't commit myself. Then another letter came from Japan: Honda had decided not to start in the small classes. I received a contract, but did not need to enter into a racing obligations. For private races, the factory gave me the five-cylinder 125, with which I had become world champion. I also had the four- and two-cylinder

> machines with which I won the title in 1964 and 1962, but also a quarter-litre machine with four cylinders.[14]

The finale of Race Week in 1966 was the Senior, held on the Friday. It was to be Hailwood's ninth TT win, but also one of his hardest as he fought arch-rival Giacomo Agostini on an MV triple, who was in fine form. Hailwood's battle was not just against Agostini – he had an entirely separate struggle with a motorcycle that was wilful and unco-operative, the four-cylinder 500cc RC181. This was a completely new design, developed alongside the 350cc RC173 that it resembled superficially. Indeed, so bad was the handling that it would hardly go in a straight line, its characteristics clearly obvious to spectators. The rival MV was less powerful but was more compact, and the Italian firm had had more time to develop it and get the handling right. It also had a torque curve that allowed it to get all of its power on to the ground more smoothly, for maximum traction. The Honda by contrast had the greater power, but its torque curve was much steeper, meaning that the massive quantities of thrust that it was capable of producing kicked in suddenly. With a small area of contact with the road provided by the narrower harder compound tyres of the day (Hailwood once described them as 'wooden tyres'), converting power to traction was less easy. Honda had used Dunlop tyres since 1964, and although the compound had changed and improved over successive years, Hailwood freely admitted that around the Isle of Man circuit he thought Avon tyres were better suited.

Mike felt that the 250cc and 350cc Honda machines were good, and he enjoyed racing them. Their inherent stability meant that he could take risks, and push things as far as he wanted without putting himself in danger. In the 250cc class the rival Yamahas might have been quicker in a straight line, but Hailwood could make up for this through his riding ability. It was a different story, however, with Honda's 500cc machine, the RC181, a six-speed 85bhp monster; riding this beast was not about trying to win, it was just trying to stay on it that was the challenge. Indeed, it was as difficult to control going into corners as it was on the straights. The reason that it was hard to handle lay in the fact that it had just a half-loop frame, almost like that of a moped, with the engine bolted on and closing the loop; the motor was intended to be a stress-bearing member and to provide strength to the whole thing, but it did nothing of the sort. Belatedly the mechanics had welded struts on to it here and there to try to provide rigidity, but it had little effect; the situation was compounded by the fact that the front brake was unduly heavy and affected the steering. Going over bumps the machine had a tendency to twist, with the back end coming around to meet the front. Hailwood remembered:

> I really enjoyed racing the 250, even though the Yamahas I raced against were quicker. The 250 was quite well behaved and easy to handle. The 350 was okay, too. When I rode it I was within my capabilities. But every time I rode the 500 I used to think, on the morning before the race, I wish I didn't have to ride in this event. I wish it wasn't on.
>
> It wasn't just the usual matter of trying to win, it was trying to stay on the thing. It really was the most frightening experience. I could stick my neck out on the 250. I could really have a go and not be worried for a second. I could dice all the way with Bill Ivy and Phil Read on their Yamahas, and even though the Honda was streets slower I enjoyed the racing. But to try anything at all on the 500 I felt I was risking my life. I had no confidence in the bike. I had to concentrate all the time on keeping

> it stable. I had trouble with it at almost every point of a circuit: into corners and out of them, on the straights, winding it on over the bumpy bits. It whipped like mad and bent in the middle. Then it wobbled all over the road ... The design was basically wrong. The instability came from the tremendous power of the engine setting up reactions through the frame. I can't understand why Honda, with all their money and technical know-how, failed to rectify that fault. It seems they had a blind spot on the question of frames. They reasoned that if they made the fastest motor in the business there was no reason why the rider shouldn't win. If the Honda got beaten they simply developed another engine with more power. They must have spent a fortune on new engines – and in all fairness they were terrific – but they failed to realise that for a fraction of the cost they could have developed a decent frame.[15]

Prior to the start of the racing season, Hailwood had taken matters into his own hands in order to try to sort out the problem with the 500 frame. He spoke first to Ken Sprayson of Renolds tubing – Sprayson was sympathetic but wasn't able to do anything in the timescale that was necessary, so he went to a contact in Italy who put something together in a couple of weeks. With a spare Honda engine in it, Mike and a friend put it through its paces at tracks in Italy and although it was an improvement on the factory frame, it was still a long way from being race ready. Matters took a turn for the worse when the press got wind of the fact that Hailwood was trying to develop his own frame. Honda were embarrassed and furious, and wrote him a strongly worded letter on the subject. They refused to allow him to use it as part of the factory team, and there the matter rested.

On the day of the 1966 Senior TT, few spectators could be in any doubt as to the challenges that Hailwood faced. As well as battling a brilliant opponent in the form of Agostini, he had another fight on his hands, against the one thing that should have been his ally – his own motorcycle. Several times on each lap Mike almost came to grief but somehow brought the beast under control. On the first lap at the bottom of Bray Hill he stood on the footrests as he wrestled to get it around the right-hander, Hailwood remembering afterwards:

> That was the hairiest ever … I thought I would have a go at taking Bray flat out … It hit the bottom with such a bump that the next thing I was heading for the wall on the far side and I had to stand up to pull it back.[16]

His friend Ted Macauley was spectating at this point and had a front-row view of this hair-raising incident:

> I was standing nearby when we heard the familiar howl of the Honda as Mike headed towards Bray, just after Pit Straight. Mike was piling it on down Bray, a steep, bumpy ski-run of a hill, at around 130 mph, when the bike began to wobble. He shot up from the saddle, stood upright on the footrests and wrestled with the handlebars, like a rough-rider trying to bring down a steer by its horns. It was a heart-stopping moment and it was all over in a flash, but it left the crowd cold with fear.[17]

Mike was on fantastic pace nevertheless, and by Kirk Michael was way ahead. During the next five laps there were many more hair-raising incidents, including touching the kerb at Union Mills, but Hailwood stormed over the Mountain, wringing every ounce of power out of the big Honda; Agostini was also having the ride of his life and stuck closely with him. Thirty-five miles out he was only six seconds behind on corrected time. On lap two Agostini broke Hailwood's 1963 lap record, in only his second ever Senior TT. This, however, pushed 'Mike the Bike' to even greater heights. He in turn put the lap record up to 107.07mph, increasing his lead over Ago to eleven seconds in the process. At half distance, Hailwood led Agostini by twenty seconds. The two teams produced near-perfect pit stops, but on lap four Agostini began to experience problems with his front brake. At every timing point Hailwood was now stretching his lead, despite rain beginning to fall on lap five. With wet roads to contend with in the second half, there were slides galore. Agostini backed off even further, no doubt remembering that he had slid off in conditions like this the previous year. Hailwood not only won in these difficult conditions but put the race average up to 103.11mph. His fifth Senior TT win created racing history by beating the four each achieved by Stanley Woods and John Surtees.

In 1966 Honda won four out of five solo races at the TT, and by the end of the season, as well as three individual rider's World Championships, the firm had won the manufacturer's World Championship in all five solo classes. It was an unprecedented achievement, and this was to be the high watermark of their 1960s Grand Prix campaign.

The finale of Honda's involvement in the Isle of Man TT would come the following year, at the sixtieth anniversary and culminated in one of the greatest races in the history of the event, which is still spoken of in reverential terms today. Honda had decided not to contest the 50cc and 125cc classes that year as they continued to divert resources to car development. Hailwood would campaign in the 250cc, 350cc and 500cc classes that season, with only the support of Ralph Bryans, an acknowledged 50cc specialist. Bryans remembered:

> I was 5ft 7in and weighed around 9st 3 or 4, so my build was right for the smaller machines. I was not involved in the testing of the larger machines at all, but I did ride the 250s in 1967 when there were only two members of the team left, Mike and I. We travelled the world together and I got to know Mike better … I think Honda were probably a little bit unfair on Mike in 1967. I am convinced they asked too much of him. It's no mean achievement winning a Grand Prix, but when you are expected to win three of them on the same day it's just not on. Undoubtedly that was the hardest year of Mike's life. I was told at the beginning, 'Ok you've got one 250, its a 1966 model and we haven't another. You've got to ride it and not break the thing.' That's a grand way to go off into a Grand Prix season … But I accepted the situation … Midway through the season … I suggested there was no point in having Mike battering his head against a brick wall – 250, 350, 500 – and I may as well move into the 350 as well as the 250 at certain Grands Prix. They agreed to that … [18]

Ted Macauley confirms that by the summer of 1967 his friend Hailwood was under more pressure, and was more nervy, than at any other time since they had first met at a party at Geoff Duke's house several years before. The first race on the Island that year was the 250cc Lightweight TT, which Hailwood won; the first of a hat-trick of wins, just ahead of British rival Phil Read. In the 250cc class there had been a fierce, season-long battle between Read and Ivy on the Yamaha fours and Hailwood and Bryans on the Honda sixes, a battle that would only be decided in the last race of the campaign. The Yamahas had been improved and were lower and more powerful; as a result they now had some 5bhp more than the Honda six. This was compensated for by the fabulous riding of Hailwood, but on very fast circuits, such as Francorchamps and Monza, the Yamahas had the advantage because of their superior speed in a straight line. In the Lightweight TT on the Monday of Race Week Hailwood led from the start, although he was hampered by the poor handling of his machine, caused by larger rear forks. These had been fitted in order to accommodate an oversized rear tyre, which it was believed would avoid excess wear. He gave a thumbs down sign as he passed the pits for the first time, indicating that all was not well, but was still six seconds ahead of Read at Ballaugh on the second lap. Mike complained to his pit crew about the poor handling during the fuel stop, but he still beat Read by over a minute, putting him on equal terms with Stanley Woods on ten TT wins. Speaking after the race, Mike was typically understated, commenting:

> The bike wasn't handling quite as well as in practice, but we managed just to stay ahead. I told them in the pits that it wasn't handling well, but there was nothing they could do about it … Phil Read was always an ever-present threat, so I pressed on a bit.[19]

Later, after the emotion had subsided, he expanded a little:

> I think [1967] was probably the hardest TT Week I have ever had I think really, because we had Phil Read and Bill Ivy on the 250 Yamahas which were considerably quicker than the Honda. We made a bit of an alteration to the tyres on the 250 which I hadn't tried in practice, which was a bit foolish of me and it was not handling very well during the race, so I just had to make the best of a bad job and

> hope for the best. [The machine] was about ten miles per hour slower than the Yamahas [so] I didn't really have any plans, I just set off and went as fast as I could to try to get a bit of a lead … Good old Nobby Clark was at Ramsey Hairpin with a signalling board and I think I was minus two seconds on Bill Ivy or something halfway round the first lap and I got up to Windy Corner and I saw him coming round the three left-handers up there. I could see him behind me, so I knew I was in the lead. As you are going round Windy Corner to the right you can see them coming down the other part of the Mountain. As I completed the first lap I was three or four seconds in the lead from Phil, and I drew slightly away from Phil all the way through the race. Well I managed to win it by a minute or something.[20]

Behind Phil Read, Ralph Bryans brought his Honda home in third place, but it had been a difficult ride for him. His front brake had given him problems from the start and he had been forced to rely on the rear unit. He also had trouble with a stiff gear change that had refused to budge, and had even torn the sole off his right boot in trying to force it to change down. When the machines were wheeled to the stripping tent for scrutineering afterwards, Hailwood's machine appeared immaculate. The larger rear tyre, despite the other problems it had caused, certainly appeared less worn than usual. The chain, brakes and clutch were all in good condition and there was no sign that the engine had regurgitated oil. Bryan's machine, by contrast, showed considerably more wear on his smaller rear tyre – the tread had actually been scuffed off the crown in places – but this was probably due to the fact he had been forced to use the rear brake more viciously than normal. Hailwood and Read would both finish the season with the same number of points in this class, but Hailwood went on to take the title, with five wins against Read's four. Ivy finished third. The manufacturers' title in this class went to Honda, followed by Yamaha, MZ and Bultaco.

Later in TT week came the Junior, with Hailwood's other rival Agostini beaten into second place. From a standing start the Englishman shattered his own absolute and race records, in a performance described as once of the most inspiring in the history of racing on the Isle of Man. Despite a slick start by Agostini, he was blown into the weeds by the Honda rider, who led him by nearly fifty seconds by the end of the first lap. Not even a superior pit stop nine seconds quicker than that of his rival could bring Agostini back into contention in this race, as Hailwood rode on through wobbles and slides. Mike had a new weapon at his disposal, in that Honda had taken the previous year's 250cc six-cylinder machine (which he felt handled better than the 350cc four-cylinder) and enlarged it for the Junior race. Mike's win was a terrific achievement: it was the first time since 1924 that a 350cc machine had broken the existing 500cc lap record, and in taking the victory Hailwood had become the most successful competitor in TT history up to that point, with eleven TT wins. On the podium after the race he was presented with the winner's garland by Stanley Woods, the man whose record he had just broken. Asked at a post-race press conference about his two opening laps at over 107mph, Hailwood was characteristically modest:

> I didn't realise I was going that fast, I was just pressing on a bit more than usual but I didn't realise it was that fast. I rolled it off a little bit when I was in the lead. The 350 is a lot easier to ride [than the 500]. I think the more power you've got round a circuit like this the more trouble you're in. You've got more useable power on the 350.[21]

Mike was equally coy about the result in another interview directly afterwards, insisting that Agostini had been holding something back for the next battle to come on the Island. Again, however, a few months later and away from the glare of press cameras, Hailwood was in a more reflective mood:

> I had had all this practice [before the race] on the 250 which is very similar to the 350 riding-wise. The frame is the same, just a bit stiffer in places, a bit heavier, and I thought well you know the best plan here is to go as fast as I could, but I didn't realise quite how fast I was going, it was ridiculous. Well it wasn't as hairy as the 250 [race], though I did have a couple of scary moments, though I was surprised it was quite so fast. Although Giacomo goes round the Island at a hell of a lick, experience and knowledge of the circuit counts; this little bit of extra knowledge means I can find these extra seconds.[22]

The stage was now set for a dramatic showdown between the two gladiators in the final race of the week. On the world stage meanwhile, with more power than the four and nearly 20kg less weight, the combination of Hailwood and Honda six was to prove so superior that Hailwood would take the 350cc title by winning the first five races of the season, and then hand the bike over to Ralph Bryans, who in turn would gather enough points during the rest of the year to end up third in the World Championship. Agostini would be second overall with the MV. Another manufacturers' title would go to Honda.

Back on the Island, however, the next race, the showpiece finale – the Diamond Senior TT – would involve the troublesome 500cc machine. Before signing a new contract with Honda for 1967, Hailwood had insisted that work should be done to improve the frame and consequently the handling. Honda had promised that they would attend to it and so Mike had signed, but no new frames ever materialised. Indeed, Honda's response to the problems Hailwood had encountered with this machine in the previous year was entirely typical of their approach – they simply increased the power of the engine. The cylinder capacity had now gone up from 489.9cc the previous year to 499.9cc this year, and power output was now nearly 90bhp at 12,000 rpm, as against 85bhp at the same revs the previous year. One of the attempts to improve handling involved mounting the front wheel in excenters, so that the trail could be altered, but by all accounts this did not bring much of an advantage. Hailwood explained later:

> It was the worst race I ever had. I was riding a camel … The 500 was a terrible handler, and if it had been a better handler I could've got round a lot quicker. I think with a better frame I could've got round easily at over 110mph. If you don't have a decent frame you can't go well at all.[23]

The afternoon of the 1967 Diamond Senior found Hailwood in his hotel room, all nervous tension as he prepared for the coming race. He pulled on a pair of navy blue ballet tights – incongruous but also invaluable for keeping him warm under his leathers. Next came a T-shirt, before struggling into the battered one-piece leathers, and black boots with holes worn by repeated contact with asphalt. The period of waiting before a race was the worst, and his hands, seeking something to occupy them, repeatedly polished the lenses of his goggles even though they were already crystal clear. The adrenalin, no matter how unpleasant, was vital in sharpening his reactions and concentration. Grabbing his pudding basin helmet, painted in the famous Hailwood racing colours of red, white and gold, and chipped and scarred by flying stones, he threw his kid leather gloves and goggles inside and set off through the hotel, towards the car park. As he did so, holidaymakers and hotel staff shouted or whispered their good wishes to him as he passed. Every single one received a 'thank you' in return. Hailwood, the most unlikely motorcycle racing champion, public school educated and the son of a millionaire, was unfailingly polite.

Arriving at the Grandstand, he was met by a gaggle of autograph hunters, but only one, a small boy, had his programme signed as Hailwood retreated deeper into his race persona. At the paddock, the air was hazy with blue smoke as a hundred machines were revved by mechanics, creating a deafening noise. Others, tyre-fitters and chain specialists, ran to and fro bringing spares, weaving between race officials with pieces of paper trying to sort out the final order of competitors. In the midst of this chaos, Hailwood and Agostini chatted unconcernedly in Italian. Suddenly all was silence. With fifteen minutes to go, engines had been cut and riders prepared to start. In the Honda pit, the chief mechanic Aika-San had organised his team so that one man held the phone, ready to relay information about Hailwood's race position from others at vital points around the circuit. Aika-San had a board ready to chalk up information for Mike. Other mechanics had their tools lined up on the pit wall, pristine white gloves at the ready, the trademark of the Honda mechanics. As the maroon sounded, and the starter's flag dropped, Hailwood was pushing the big machine down Glencrutchery Road until it roared into life. The ubiquitous presence of Mike's father Stan hovered opposite the scoreboard, watching the dial turn to indicate his son's progress around the famous 37¾-mile course. Murray Walker's autobiography sums up this phenomenal race and captures some of the tension and atmosphere beforehand:

> The TT always seemed to rise to the occasion and the 1967 Golden Jubilee Senior race was truly an unforgettable race of the Titans. Just consider the scenario: there was the 27-year-old Mike Hailwood, Master of the Isle of Man and a racing phenomenon, and his great Italian rival Giacomo Agostini, also the son of a millionaire, whose swarthy film-star looks, cheerful personality and riding brilliance made him almost as popular with the crowds as his English rival … I was at the nerve centre of the BBC's coverage of the TT, the main commentary box at the Grandstand, looking straight down on the starting grid in ideal weather. In rather tatty old leathers, Hailwood, No. 4, bump-started the Honda into life and blasted off down steep Bray Hill at enormous velocity, followed 30 seconds later by No. 9, Agostini. The other 37 competitors might not have existed for all the attention that they got: it was all focussed on the two superstars. In the main Grandstand on the Glencrutchery Road everyone's eyes were fixed on the scoreboard indicator clocks that show where all the riders are on the 37.73-mile lap; stopwatches were working overtime to record the time gaps between the two rivals at the various check points.[24]

Assistant Press Officer Neil Hanson was actually in the pit lane between the Honda and MV crews that afternoon, in order to provide pit stop timings for the press box in the Grandstand above. In all of his years of involvement with the TT races, he ranked that event as one of the most dramatic and memorable. He remembered:

> The atmosphere was very excited – the fight was fantastic, the outcome impossible to predict … I was supporting Hailwood. I think the extra speed of the Honda did not compensate fully for its bad handling so he was the underdog.[25]

Murray Walker's frantic description of the 1967 Diamond Senior TT as it unfolded captures all the drama of what would be Mike Hailwood's twelfth TT victory, his eleventh win earlier in the week making him at that time the most successful rider in TT history:

> … and leading on the road on lap two Hailwood well out in front three laps gone, half distance, and pit stop time. Hailwood's mechanic signalling Mike where to stop and here's the Honda – start the watches, this pit stop's going to be absolutely crucial, for Hailwood's cut Agostini's lead to a mere two seconds so this could win or lose the race for Mike, goggles changed fuel still going in, and there's Agostini, what a sight – the first two refueling next to each other, but Mike's in trouble he's frantically hammering up a loose twist grip, this could change everything, so Mike's been lapping at over a hundred and eight with a sloppy throttle control – fantastic – but now this pit stop's losing him valuable time. He's away – his stop 47.8 seconds, now what about Agostini's time for all this, he's off after 37 seconds so as he starts his fourth lap Agostini by twelve seconds but with a hundred and thirteen miles still to go, and there's Agostini howling along the Veranda on lap 4 still leading Hailwood by a clear twelve seconds and averaging nearly a hundred and seven including his pit stop. This is what makes the TT course what it is: the Mountain Road; mile after mile past the Bungalow and

> Windy corner on past the lonely 33rd Milestone to Keppel Gates then down the terrifying drop to the Creg and the waiting crowds.
>
> Ramsey – Hailwood through Parliament Square to start the Mountain climb for the fifth time. Agostini 31 seconds later, so Hailwood's leading for the first time by one second and here's Agostini thirty seconds behind, so on corrected time it's a dead heat again, with only forty-five miles to go. On to Signpost Corner, lap five, Hailwood another lap at almost a hundred and eight and now the countdown for Agostini. Thirty seconds, forty, he's late, long overdue, Ago must be out, yes at Governor's Bridge Peter Williams arrives in second place. Agostini is out, coasting with a broken chain, and he's got off the course onto the slip road at Governors, what cruel luck; but the last lap for Mike Hailwood is no cruise home to victory for that twist grip's loose again and his lap speed's right down, but while the others ride on poor Agostini coasts in, and tries to continue, only to be excluded through turning off the course at Governors. Bitter disappointment for poor Ago and his face shows it. So it's victory again for Mike Hailwood, a magnificent victory but victory partly through the misfortune of a brilliant rival and not the way Mike, great sportsman that he is, likes to win.[26]

In fact, Hailwood's outright lap record set that day would stand for eight years, and would not be beaten until 1975 when it was finally topped by Mick Grant and his all-conquering Kawasaki. Hailwood was frank about the fact that he had not expected to win before the race, and was certain that he would not have done so if Agostini had not gone out. His frantic hammering of the throttle in the pits had been an attempt to splay the end over to hold it on, but it had not worked and it kept sliding down. Every time it slid down he had to hoik it up, and spent more time watching the handlebars than watching the road. He told reporters afterwards:

> I was lucky. If Agostini's chain had not broken I don't think I could have won. That second lap was just about as fast as I could go. I made up quite a bit of time but lost it at the pit stop when I had to fix the throttle. The throttle started to work loose again on the fifth lap and on the last lap I was riding virtually one-handed. In fact, I almost had to stop once to push it back on again and was holding it on for most of the lap.[27]

At the Grandstand he elaborated further:

> It was very hectic, very hairy, and much too fast. I found out that Agostini was out when somebody stuck a signal out down by Hawthorn Inn there – one of the fans – I thought he might be spooking me so I slowed down. I rolled off from 107 to 100 mph on the last lap – I had no choice actually as my throttle kept falling off. Had Giacomo kept going, well he'd have won.[28]

That evening, Hailwood took Agostini out to enjoy the nightlife of the Isle of Man and cheer him up; it was after all the Italian's twenty-fifth birthday that day! Agostini, despite his disappointment on the Island, went on to take the 500cc World Championship in 1967. At the end of the season, both riders had the same number of points and both had five wins; Hailwood had two second placings, but Agostini had three seconds and so became World Champion, with Hailwood second and John Hartle (Matchless) third. This was a bitter blow for Honda, who had now made two attempts to secure the most prestigious prize in motorcycle racing, the 500cc riders' World Championship, and had failed each time (although they had secured the 500cc constructor's title in 1966). Hailwood summed things up with a typically generous tribute to the rider who had become his greatest rival, indeed the 'Hailwood-Agostini era' at the TT is still talked of in glowing terms today by commentators and fans, who recognise that it was a golden age for the event:

> Despite all their investment, effort and ambition, Honda had failed to win the solo championship which meant more than any other in terms of prestige and showroom sales, but for my part I never felt that I couldn't beat Ago, given equal machinery. The Italian's great strength was his consistency, and with the MV Agusta he had the more reliable machine in our epic duels in 1965 and 1966, but he was a worthy champion and became the most successful motor-cycle racer of all … for two years we battled for the 500cc crown. It was a head-on fight at one grand prix after another, and although you can't afford to be too charitable to other riders in motor-cycle racing, the rivalry was good humoured enough and we got on well together.[29]

By now, the company's attention was elsewhere, as they sought to develop a car with which they could compete successfully in Formula 1, and prove their ability in the four-wheeled world as they had in two. The race squad obviously believed that any suspension of activity would only be a temporary one, as directly after the 1967 TT Aika-San told British reporters that he believed Luigi Taveri would be rejoining a revitalised squad:

> We will be racing in all classes at the Japanese GP at Fisco in October with new machines ridden by Luigi Taveri and Ralph Bryans. Next year we will compete in all classes and Honda hopes that Mike Hailwood will ride for us again. We may also get a second rider for the bigger classes.[30]

Yet it was not to be. Honda withdrew from Grand Prix motorcycle racing completely, but paid Hailwood £50,000 not to ride for any of their competitors in 1968 at World Championship events. They did, however, allow him to keep three of his machines including the 1966 350cc, and the 500cc machine on which he had won the 1967 Senior, along with enough parts such as spare pistons and gaskets to keep them in running order. This was on condition that he only used them to contest non-championship National and International races – these were attractive because they traditionally paid more start money than Grand Prix races, which riders had to attend for the championship points, and were therefore a more lucrative prospect. Pauline Hailwood remembered:

> Mike [only] trusted Nobby [Clark]. When Honda pulled out of racing in 1967 they gave Mike three bikes for private meetings and Nobby looked after them. In fact, he lived with Mike in Heston and they had a garage round the back.[31]

Around 1970 John Cooper phoned Mike and asked if he could borrow the 500cc Honda for some UK meetings. He agreed and told Cooper to head down to the garage at Heston where Nobby Clark would set it up for him. Hailwood warned him about its handling characteristics, but Cooper was initially dismissive. He took it to Snetterton for a twenty-lap race, where he found that although it was incredibly fast on the straights it was almost impossible to steer around corners. Cooper commented memorably:

> When you say Mike Hailwood's bike taught me a thing or two, well it taught me that only Hailwood could ride it … Next time I saw it it was locked up in the Donington Museum and that's where it ought to stop … I find it unbelievable, quite unbelievable that he got it round the Island. I can't believe that he ever raced that bike and I saw him do it … He deserves the bloody VC.[32]

It was one of these machines that was auctioned at the major sale of Hailwood family memorabilia conducted by Coys of Kensington in 1997. The machine was purchased by motorcycling components dealer Bob Heath, and has been paraded at numerous events in the years since. It was his frustration at being effectively barred from top-level motorcycle competition that led Hailwood eventually into car racing and to Formula 1.

Soichiro Honda spoke at a press conference in Paris in 1968, in which he also stated that the withdrawal from top-level motorcycle racing was only temporary. However, the firm did not field a motorcycle with full factory backing again until they unveiled the NR ('New Racer') model at the British Grand Prix at Silverstone in 1979.

Aside from the World Championships, lap records and other achievements, one of the greatest legacies of the Honda years in the 1960s was the camaraderie that grew up between the team members. Luigi Taveri reflected shortly before his death that among his greatest memories were of:

> … the lasting friendship within racing sport with riders like Mike Hailwood, Ralph Bryans or Jim Redman. But

> also the personal friendship with the family of the Honda founder Soichiro Honda remains in my recollection. After my resignation I was invited by Soichiro Honda with my whole family to Japan where an unforgettable resignation party took place. Up to his death Soichiro Honda never forgot that I have contributed a little to making his name famous all over the world. Still today the company every year makes available to me on loan a new Honda machine.[33]

Taveri summed up what it took to be a World Champion motorcycle racer:

> Absolute passion, complete devotion, iron discipline, technical understanding, the unconditional will, in itself to work, training diligence, above-average reaction times, renunciation of niceties, the greatest sporting ambition ...[34]

Every one of the men who raced Honda's awesome machines in the 1960s had these attributes in spades, whether or not they had the good fortune (and it must be admitted that there is a good deal of fortune in racing success) to hold a world title as a result of their efforts. These machines, when combined with a circuit that has as much character as the Isle of Man TT course, produced a golden age in motorcycle racing history. Jim Redman returned after twelve years away to see Mike Hailwood's 1978 comeback, and toured the course in a car:

> In the Sixties we had a lot of battles together and I beat him now and then. But it was the old Honda versus MV story. I was on Hondas and they were lighter, lower, shorter and faster. They didn't handle so well but they

gave me enough speed to beat Mike. I made no secret of it that on equal bikes I wouldn't have beaten him. But that's no disgrace because he's the best!

Doing that lap after 12 years away was a nostalgic time. Every mile brought a memory back to me – of trying to follow Bob McIntyre through the Thirteenth and nearly coming unstuck; of the Honda's leaping and bucking over the bumps; of [Australian rider] Jack Ahearn suggesting, in his incredibly dry way, that the answer to the handling problem on a particular corner might be to close the throttle slightly! I always tried to stay at the same boarding house as Jack. He has a fantastic sense of humour and you could bet on plenty of laughs.[35]

EPILOGUE

When Honda appeared for the first time on the Isle of Man in 1959, no one could have foreseen the impact that this obscure Japanese brand would have on the motorcycle world in general, and the Grand Prix racing scene in particular. They caused a revolution in racing motorcycle design, and paved the way for their Japanese competitors – Suzuki in 1960 and Yamaha in 1961, followed later by Kawasaki. Year after year the number of cylinders rose to enable higher engine speeds and hence higher power output. Had they continued racing, there would probably have been a 50cc triple, a 125cc six, and a 250cc V8. Alas, it was not to be. After nine successful years, sixteen World Championships and 138 Grand Prix victories, Honda had achieved their goal, and retired from GP racing.

Their influence on engine design was profound. When they arrived in the Isle of Man with four-valve cylinder heads, the prevailing opinion was that the Japanese were rather behind the times – four-valve heads had been used extensively in Europe, and had shown no advantage over two-valve heads. But when Honda started winning with that 'outdated' model, those voices from the European 'experts' were silenced. Benelli was the first to take a leaf out of Honda's book and converted their 250cc four to four valves – which gave them an increase in power of 5bhp and brought an end to their recurring problem of valve breakage. They were soon followed by MV Agusta and Jawa. Sometimes wondrous things are claimed for the Honda engines of the 1960s, for example that they contained rare metals never used before or since. The truth is that Honda were successful because they were prepared to innovate and experiment. Not all of their designs were successful, and often they won because their engines struck just the right balance between positive and negative design aspects. But using the TT as their test bed, their technicians introduced improvements in automotive technology that had worldwide benefits.

More than this, they helped to rehabilitate the Japanese, particularly in British eyes, following the events of the Second World War, earning a legion of fans in Europe and America. They also accelerated the end of the once-dominant British motorcycle industry, which was both unable and unwilling to introduce new ideas and new working practices. Though clever marketing, and slogans like 'You meet the nicest people on a Honda', they portrayed motorcycling as fun and safe, and steered it away from the image it had developed in the 1950s as the preserve of greasy rockers and Hell's Angels.

The Isle of Man holds a hallowed place in the history of the Honda company, for so much was achieved there in those eight years of intense competition. Long may it remain thus.

NOTES

Chapter One

1. Anon, *A Look at Honda.*
2. Op cit.
3. Op cit.
4. Op cit.
5. Op cit.
6. Op cit.
7. Tetsuo Sakiya, *Honda Motor: The Men, the Management, the Machines*, p.110.
8. Sakiya, op cit, p.111.
9. *100 Greatest TT Moments*, Duke Marketing, 2007, author's transcript.
10. Kevin Cameron, *Cycle World*, 10 March 2022.
11. Sakiya, op cit, p.112.
12. Ibid., p.113.
13. Naomi Taniguchi interview – author's collection.
14. Op cit.
15. *100 Greatest TT Moments*, Duke Marketing, 2007, author's transcript.
16. *Isle of Man Daily Times*, 10 February 1959.
17. Taniguchi, op cit.
18. https://global.honda/heritage/episodes/1958manttrace.html
19. Taniguchi, op cit.
20. Op cit.
21. https://global.honda/heritage/episodes/1958manttrace.html

22. Op cit.
23. Op cit.
24. Roy Moore, correspondence with author.
25. Adrian Earnshaw, correspondence with author.
26. *Isle of Man Daily Times*, 2 June 1959.
27. Taniguchi, op cit.
28. https://global.honda/heritage/episodes/1958manttrace.html
29. *Motorcycling*, 11 June 1959.
30. Translation provided by Don Simons.
31. Taniguchi, op cit.
32. Ibid.

Chapter Two

1. *TT Special*, 15 June 1960, p.18.
2. Jim Redman, *Six Times World Motorcycle Champion; the autobiography*, p.98.
3. Redman, op cit, p.97.
4. Luigi Taveri, *Mein Leben auf Zwei Rädern*, p.104 (author's translation).
5. *Sound Stories TT 1961*, Stanley Schofield Productions, author's transcript.
6. Stan Hailwood, *The Hailwood Story*, p.24.
7. Taveri, op cit, p.107.
8. Stan Hailwood, *op cit*, p.25.
9. Mike Hailwood, *The Art of Motorcycle Racing*, p.166.
10. http://murraysmotorcycles.weebly.com/history.html
11. *Sound Stories TT 1961*, Stanley Schofield Productions, author's transcript.
12. Op cit.
13. Bob McIntyre, *Motor Cycling Today*, p.65.
14. *Sound Stories TT 1961*, Stanley Schofield Productions, author's transcript.

15. McIntyre, op cit, p.53.
16. Mike Hailwood, op cit, p.169.
17. *Sound Stories TT 1964–1968*, Stanley Schofield Productions, author's transcript.
18. Ted Macauley, *Hailwood*, p.38.
19. Macauley, op cit.
20. *Daily Mirror*, 23 June 1961.
21. Taniguchi, op cit.

Chapter Three

1. *Sound Stories TT 1962*, Stanley Schofield Productions, author's transcript.
2. Op cit.
3. Op cit.
4. Derek Minter, *Racing All My Life*, p.95.
5. Op cit, p.96.
6. Tommy Robb, correspondence with author.
7. *Sound Stories TT 1962*, Stanley Schofield Productions, author's transcript.
8. Taveri, *op cit*, p.19.
9. Hugh Anderson, *Being There*, p.133.
10. *Sound Stories TT 1962*, Stanley Schofield Productions, author's transcript.
11. Op cit.
12. Tommy Robb, *TT to Tokyo*, p.51.
13. *Sound Stories TT 1963*, Stanley Schofield Productions, author's transcript.
14. Jim Redman, *Wheels of Fortune*, p.63.
15. *Motor Cycle News*, 12 June 1963.
16. *Sound Stories TT 1963*, Stanley Schofield Productions, author's transcript.
17. Op cit.
18. Op cit.

19. Op cit.
20. Op cit.
21. Robb, op cit, p.52.
22. Taveri, op cit, p.127.
23. Miles Cowsill, *Realising the Dream at the TT*, p56.

Chapter Four

1. Taveri, op cit, p.142.
2. Redman, *Wheels of Fortune*, p.59.
3. Redman, op cit.
4. *Sound Stories TT 1964*, Stanley Schofield Productions, author's transcript.
5. Op cit.
6. *Octane*, October 2006.
7. www.bonhams.com
8. *Sound Stories TT 1964*, Stanley Schofield Productions, author's transcript.
9. *Motor Cycling*, 20 June 1964.
10. Op cit.
11. Op cit.
12. Taveri, op cit, p.153.
13. Ibid., p.154.
14. *Sound Stories TT 1964*, Stanley Schofield Productions, author's transcript.
15. Op cit.
16. Op cit.
17. Op cit.
18. Op cit.
19. Redman, *Wheels of Fortune*, p.61.
20. *Motor Cycling*, 19 June 1965.
21. *Sound Stories TT 1965*, Stanley Schofield Productions, author's transcript.
22. Op cit.

23. Op cit.
24. Op cit.
25. Taveri, op cit, p.181.
26. *Sound Stories TT 1965,* Stanley Schofield Productions, author's transcript.
27. *Motor Cycling,* 26 June 1965.
28. Taveri, op cit, p.182.
29. *Motor Cycle News,* 9 June 1965.

Chapter Five

1. Macauley, op cit, p.81.
2. *Motor Cycling,* 11 September 1965.
3. Mike Hailwood, *Bikes,* p.33.
4. Macauley, op cit, p.79.
5. *Sound Stories TT 1966,* Stanley Schofield Productions, author's transcript.
6. *Motor Cycling,* 3 September 1966.
7. *Motorcycle News,* 31 August 1966.
8. Cowsill, op cit, p.59.
9. *Sound Stories TT 1966,* Stanley Schofield Productions, author's transcript.
10. Op cit.
11. Taveri, op cit, p.210.
12. *Sound Stories TT 1966,* Stanley Schofield Productions, author's transcript.
13. Taveri, op cit, p.210.
14. Taveri, op cit.
15. Macauley, op cit, p.76.
16. *Motor Cycle News,* 7 September 1966.
17. Macauley, op cit, p.79.
18. Christopher Hilton, *A Man called Mike,* p.125.
19. *Sound Stories TT 1967,* Stanley Schofield Productions, author's transcript.

20. *Sound Stories TT 1964–1968*, Stanley Schofield Productions, author's transcript.
21. *Sound Stories TT 1967*, Stanley Schofield Productions, author's transcript.
22. *Sound Stories TT 1964–1968*, Stanley Schofield Productions, author's transcript.
23. Op cit.
24. Murray Walker, *Unless I'm Very Much Mistaken*, p.125.
25. Neil Hanson, correspondence with author.
26. *Diamond Senior*, Duke Marketing, author's transcript.
27. *Motor Cycle News*, 21 June 1967.
28. *Sound Stories TT 1967*, Stanley Schofield Productions, author's transcript.
29. Mike Hailwood, *Bikes*, p.52.
30. *Motor Cycle News*, 14 June 1967.
31. *Bikesport News*, 19 December 2017.
32. Hilton, op cit, p.127.
33. *Weltwoche* Nr. 18.09.
34. Op cit.
35. *Motor Cycle Weekly*, 17 June 1978.

BIBLIOGRAPHY

Anderson, Hugh, *Being There*, New Zealand, 2017

Anon, *A Look at Honda*, no location, no date

Ayton, C.J., *The Great Japanese Motorcycles*, New York, 1981

Cameron, Kevin, *Classic Motorcycle Race Engines: expert technical analysis of the world's great power units* Haynes, Sparkford, 2012

Cowsill, Miles, *Realising the Dream at the TT* Ramsey, Isle of Man, 2009

Hailwood, Mike, *Bikes: thirty years and more of the motor-cycle world championships*, Sevenoaks, Kent, 1982

Hailwood, Mike and Walker, Murray, *The Art of Motorcycle Racing*, London, 1963

Hailwood, Stan, *The Hailwood Story: My Son Mike*, Peterborough, 1966

Hilton, Christopher, *A Man Called Mike*, Croydon, 1992

Macauley, Ted and Hailwood, Mike, *Hailwood*, London, 1969

McIntyre, Bob, *Motor Cycling Today*, London, 1962

Minter, Derek, *Racing All My Life*, London, 1965

Redman, Jim, *Jim Redman: Six Times World Motorcycle Champion; the Autobiography*, Dorchester, Dorset 2006

Redman, Jim, *Wheels of Fortune*, London, 1966

Richardson, Matthew, *TT Titans*, Barnsley, 2018

Robb, Tommy, *TT to Tokyo*, Douglas, Isle of Man, 1974

Sakiya, Tetsuo, *Honda Motor: The Men, the Management, the Machines*, Kodansha International, New York, 1982

Taveri, Luigi, *Mein Leben auf Zwei Rädern*, Stuttgart, 1969

Walker, Murray, *Unless I'm Very Much Mistaken: My autobiography*, London, 2002

INDEX